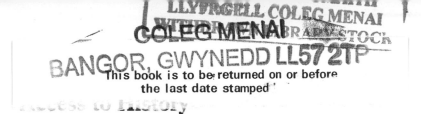

Access to History

General Editor: Keith Randell

# Napoleon, France and Europe

## Access to History

General Editor: Keith Randell

# Napoleon, France and Europe

Andrina Stiles

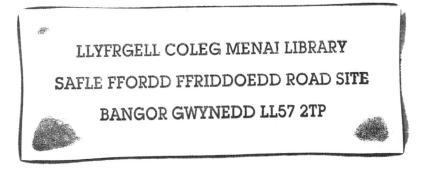

Hodder & Stoughton

A MEMBER OF THE HODDER HEADLINE GROUP

*The cover illustration shows a portrait of Napoleon by Ingres (Courtesy Musée de Liege/
Bridgeman Art Library)*

*Some other titles in the series:*

| | |
|---|---|
| **France in Revolution**<br>Duncan Townson | ISBN 0 340 53494 X |
| **France 1814–70: Monarchy, Republic and Empire**<br>Keith Randell | ISBN 0 340 51805 7 |
| **Rivalry and Accord: International Relations 1814–70**<br>John Lowe | ISBN 0 340 51806 6 |
| **The Unification of Germany 1815–90**<br>Andrina Stiles | ISBN 0 340 51810 3 |
| **The Unification of Italy 1815–70**<br>Andrina Stiles | ISBN 0 340 51809 X |
| **Habsburgs and Hohenzollerns 1713–86**<br>Walter Oppenheim | ISBN 0 340 55045 7 |

*British Library Cataloguing in Publication Data*

Stiles, Andrina
  Napoleon, France and Europe. – (Access
  to History Series)
  I. Title II. Series
  944.05
  ISBN 0–340–57375–9

First published 1993

Impression number 10  9  8  7  6  5  4  3  2
Year               1998  1997  1996  1995  1994

Typeset by Wearset, Boldon, Tyne and Wear
Printed in Great Britain for Hodder & Stoughton Educational, a division of Hodder
Headline Plc, 338 Euston Road, London, NW1 3BH by Page Bros, Norwich.

# Contents

# Preface

## To the general reader

Although the *Access to History* series has been designed with the needs of students studying the subject at higher examination levels very much in mind, it also has a great deal to offer the general reader. The main body of the text (i.e. ignoring the Study Guides at the ends of chapters) forms a readable and yet stimulating survey of a coherent topic as studied by historians. However, each author's aim has not merely been to provide a clear explanation of what happened in the past (to interest and inform): it has also been assumed that most readers wish to be stimulated into thinking further about the topic and to form opinions of their own about the significance of the events that are described and discussed (to be challenged). Thus, although no prior knowledge of the topic is expected on the reader's part, she or he is treated as an intelligent and thinking person throughout. The author tends to share ideas and possibilities with the reader, rather than passing on numbers of so-called 'historical truths'.

## To the student reader

There are many ways in which the series can be used by students studying History at a higher level. It will, therefore, be worthwhile thinking about your own study strategy before you start your work on this book. Obviously, your strategy will vary depending on the aim you have in mind, and the time for study that is available to you.

If, for example, you want to acquire a general overview of the topic in the shortest possible time, the following approach will probably be the most effective:

1   Read chapter 1 and think about its contents.
2   Read the 'Making notes' section at the end of chapter 2 and decide whether it is necessary for you to read this chapter.
3   If it is, read the chapter, stopping at each heading or ★ to note down the main points that have been made.
4   Repeat stage 2 (and stage 3 where appropriate) for all the other chapters.

If, however, your aim is to gain a thorough grasp of the topic, taking however much time is necessary to do so, you may benefit from carrying out the same procedure with each chapter, as follows:

1   Read the chapter as fast as you can, and preferably at one sitting.
2   Study the flow diagram at the end of the chapter, ensuring that you understand the general 'shape' of what you have just read.

3   Read the 'Making notes' section (and the 'Answering essay questions' section, if there is one) and decide what further work you need to do on the chapter.

4   Attempt the 'Source-based questions' section. It will sometimes be sufficient to think through your answers, but additional understanding will often be gained by forcing yourself to write them down.

When you have finished the main chapters of the book, study the 'Further Reading' section and decide what additional reading (if any) you will do on the topic.

This book has been designed to help make your studies both enjoyable and successful. If you can think of ways in which this could have been done more effectively, please write to tell me. In the meantime, I hope that you will gain greatly from your study of History.

Keith Randell

# CHAPTER 1

# Napoleon – an Introduction

On 18–19 Brumaire in the year VIII of the Revolution (9–10 November 1799) a *coup-d'état* in Paris unexpectedly brought a young General, Napoleon Bonaparte, to power in France. In the event it also led to him assuming power in most of the rest of Europe during the course of the next 15 years.

Who was he and what was he like, this man who was to dominate Europe until 1815, and to live on in the Legend after his death?

## 1 Napoleon the Man

### a) His Background

In August 1769 at Ajaccio on the island of Corsica Napoleon was born a French subject, but only just, for Corsica had been part of the Republic of Genoa until the previous year when it was ceded to France. The Buonaparte family was petty nobility with a fierce, independent pride in all that was Corsican, and at first Napoleon's father was a bitter opponent of the foreign French occupation. Before long, though, he accepted an amnesty and changed sides, seeing advantages to be gained for his growing family of five sons and three daughters by attaching himself to the French administration of the island. One of the advantages he obtained was the documentary proof of nobility he needed in order to send Napoleon, his second son, to be educated at the French government's expense at a military academy on the mainland. Fortunately perhaps for Napoleon, the Corsican nobility was considered by most Frenchmen to be much inferior in status to that of France, and his name was never entered in the '*ci-devant*' (former aristocrat) lists at the time of the Revolution.

At the age of nine the young Napoleon, whose first language was Italian, was given a crash course in French to prepare him for his future career. He never lost his Italian accent, though, and never learnt to write French grammatically – this latter fact may have been an unadmitted reason why he always dictated official documents and correspondence (see page 2), leaving it to his secretaries to correct the grammar. It is difficult to know how far he ever felt himself to be truly French, however much he spoke of 'France, first and always'. Some historians go so far as to suggest that France for him was never *la patrie* – that he was always, at least emotionally, a Corsican. It is certainly true that he initially thought of the Revolution as an opportunity for the Corsicans to gain freedom from France as they had once dreamed of gaining freedom from Genoa, and for a while he was obsessed with Rousseau's 'presentiment that this little island will one day astonish

Europe'. Later, when Corsica ceased to dominate his thoughts in the same way and he had denounced Rousseau as 'a madman', the Corsican sense of family loyalty remained with him.

Napoleon studied first at a preparatory school in France, before going on to the École Militaire in Paris where he graduated, not especially well, as a sub-lieutenant of artillery in 1785. For the next four years he continued his training as an artillery officer, while at the same time managing to spend a good deal of time in Corsica. There he came to the notice of an influential politician, whose patronage undoubtedly helped his early career, and whose mistress, Josephine, Napoleon later married. In the years between 1789 and 1792, with the emigration of as many as 6000 noble commissioned officers, there were plenty of opportunities for able and energetic, but not particularly well-born or well-endowed career-soldiers, to advance rapidly up the ladder of promotion in a way undreamed of under the Ancien Régime. A wholehearted supporter of the Revolution from its beginning in 1789, Napoleon was one of the ambitious young men to be quickly promoted. By 1793 at the age of 24 he was already a brigadier-general.

## b)  His Character

Napoleon's character was a complex one. With friends he could be charming and amusing – 'no one could be more fascinating, when he chose'. But he did not always choose, and his rages and his cold displeasure could be terrifying to those around him. He recognised the fact that his mood could change suddenly: 'I am two different men', he once said of himself.

It is a historical cliché that Napoleon was unusually short – the 'Little Corporal' of contemporary cartoons – and that his superabundant energy and overweening ambition are explained by a need to compensate for his lack of inches. Energetic and ambitious he may have been, but at a time when the standard height for adult enrolment in the French army was five feet, reduced by 1813 to four feet nine inches, Napoleon at five feet two inches was in fact above average height for a Frenchman. Very intelligent and full of vitality, he was, for much of his adult life, a workaholic, sometimes working 18 or more hours a day. His handwriting was indecipherable – it could not, he said, keep up with his thoughts so fast did ideas come to him – and he normally dictated his official communications to a half a dozen secretaries at once. It has been estimated that he 'wrote' more than 80,000 documents during his 15 years in power. Because he lived on his nerves he sometimes became anxious and fearful – especially in crowds, or when called upon to speak in public (which he did very badly). At such times he seems to have suffered from nervous collapses akin to epilepsy.

In 1796 after winning the battle of Lodi during his first Italian campaign (see page 20) he realised, he said, that he was a superior being destined to perform great things, and this belief in his 'destiny' remained with him as a driving force. He openly acknowledged that his ambition was unlimited. Whether it was as he often said ambition for France, to make her feared, respected and ruler of the world, or whether it was a similar ambition for himself, remains a matter of dispute. Military historians vary in their judgement of Napoleon's abilities as a general (see page 43), but whatever the verdict on his strategy and tactics, there is no doubt about his charismatic powers of leadership.

From 1807 onwards officials, friends and servants noticed a change in Napoleon, which became more marked after the return from Moscow in 1812. The Russian campaign (see page 28) seemed to have affected both his mental and physical health. His previously excellent memory began to decline, he became more imperious and intolerant of others' points of view and more brutally contemptuous of the rest of the human race – 'Power comes through fear', he said at this time. He began to put on weight, becoming lethargic and slow, and ageing prematurely into the balding, paunchy figure beloved of cartoonists then and since (see page 124).

## c)  His Career 1796–1815 – a Preview

However, in the 1790s, Napoleon was still slim and active, although not particularly prepossessing in appearance according to eyewitness accounts. These describe him as untidily, almost shabbily dressed, with lank, greasy shoulder-length hair and a sallow complexion. A rather serious young man, he had little sense of humour and seldom laughed. In March 1796 two events of great importance in his life occurred – he married the widowed society beauty, Josephine de Beauhearnais, and he was appointed commander of the Army of Italy. It was as a result of his military successes (see pages 20–23) in Italy (1796–7) and afterwards in Egypt (1798–9) that in 1799 he came to power in the *coup d'état* of Brumaire (see chapter 2) which made him First Consul and undisputed ruler of France.

### i)  Domestic Affairs

As First Consul (1799–1804) and then as Emperor until 1814, Napoleon's government was highly centralised and his authority as sole ruler of France was not effectively disputed. His régime was basically a dictatorship, although, despite the fact that the head of state was also head of the armed forces, it was not a military one (see page 93). By a mixture of bribery (through the liberal use of gifts of land, titles, official appointments and money to buy support), and of a ruthless suppression of freedom of thought, word and deed (through the equally liberal use of indoctrination, intimidation and propaganda to make opposition impossibly difficult), Napoleon maintained himself in power for 14 years (see chapter 3, pages 74–93).

### ii) Foreign Affairs

Foreign affairs for Napoleonic France were indistinguishable from war. Apart from the short period of peace in 1802–3 France was almost continuously at war under Napoleon. Indeed, the Peace of Amiens (1802) can be seen as little more than a truce in a long succession of wars begun under the Revolution and continued under Napoleon, which were fought by France against a succession of European coalition armies. Until 1807 Napoleon led France to a series of brilliant victories (see pages 36–47) on land, extending the French frontiers far beyond their 'natural' limits of the Rhine, the Alps and the Pyrenees, into Germany and Italy. At the beginning of 1811 the Empire reached its greatest extent, but its collapse was already threatened by the ill-fated Spanish conflict begun in 1807 (see page 25) and made certain by the ill-judged invasion of Russia in 1812 (see page 28). Even Napoleon's most strenuous efforts failed to save the Empire in the campaign of 1813 (see page 31) and with the fall of Paris to the Allies in March 1814 he was forced to abdicate, and was exiled to Elba (an island off the Italian coast). His return to France the following year (the Hundred Days) and his defeat at Waterloo marked the end of his public life (see page 34).

### iii) St Helena and After

Exiled again in 1815, this time to St Helena (a remote island in the south Atlantic from which escape proved impossible), Napoleon occupied the remaining years of his life – he died, most probably of cancer of the stomach, in 1821 shortly before his 52nd birthday – in dictating his own version of events to a group of companions on the island. From these records, and from the accumulated propaganda of his years in power, was constructed the Napoleonic Legend (see chapter 8).

## 2 Napoleon – Historical Issues

This book is concerned with Napoleon's rise and fall; with the military, political, social, cultural and economic effects, both long term and short term, on those who came under his control at home and abroad; with the reasons for his success and for his eventual failure, and with the development of the 'Napoleonic Legend'.

He was the supreme egoist: 'Himself is the only man he recognises – all other beings are mere cyphers', as one who knew him well remarked. Self-interest, he freely admitted, was his guide in all things. No one could with impunity thwart his plans – not even his first wife, Josephine, who was probably the only person he ever loved apart from himself. Contemporaries regarded him as amoral, a man to whom the usual epithets of good or bad were not applicable, who felt neither love nor hate, and who dispensed favours and kindness only in proportion to the usefulness of the recipient. He was not personally cruel – merely indifferent to the sufferings of others. They were only of value as they served his purpose – expendable when they did not. Why he lavished so much largesse on his mostly unpleasant and ungrateful relatives – he made four brothers and three brothers-in-law into kings or princes – is not entirely clear. Some historians see it as an expression of his dynastic ambition to found a European royal house of Bonaparte to rival the Habsburgs and outshine the Bourbons; others see it as due to the Corsican sense of family clannishness which never left him. Nor did the Corsican tradition of the vendetta, which he called upon to justify – at least to himself – the judicial murder in 1804 of the Duc d'Enghien, who was said to have been involved in a plot to assassinate him (see page 80).

For two centuries novelists, biographers, artists, playwrights, and lately film-makers, have all found material for their talents in depicting the life and times of Napoleon. Their views on him have usually been unsubtly polarised    the great soldier and strong ruler unjustly exiled, or the evil dictator well nicknamed the 'Ogre' and deservedly banished. Until after the Second World War even historians, caught up in the old historical assumption that events were dictated almost exclusively by the actions of powerful personalities – the 'great man' school of thought – concentrated on analysing Napoleon's personal contribution to European history, and declared it to have been either 'good' or 'bad'. This is very clearly brought out by the Dutch historian Geyl in his 'for and against' synthesis of the views of nineteenth and early twentieth century French historians on Napoleon's achievements. All of them based their conclusions on detailed studies of Napoleon, the man. This in itself presented a problem, for it can be argued that there were two Napoleons – the living one and the one of the Legend. Chapter 8 of this book looks at the Legend, how it developed and how far, if at all, it can be taken at face value.

With a lessening of interest in the personal aspects of Napoleon's career, historical research on the period has moved since the 1960s into other areas. As a result, doubt has been cast on a number of long cherished beliefs. In important reassessments of Napoleon as a soldier it has been shown that Napoleon was by no means deserving of the title of 'the greatest military leader of all time' which has so often been accorded to him, for many of his campaigns were bungled and his success dependent on the even greater incompetence of his enemies. Recent investigations into the social, cultural and economic history of the period have suggested that there was a much greater continuity with the past than was once thought, and that the extent of changes in Napoleonic society in France and in the Empire has been exaggerated. In the same way the idea of Napoleon as a radical reformer in his early domestic policies (the 'Consular miracle' of 1800–2) has come in for considerable reappraisal.

These new ideas are discussed in chapters 3, 4, 5, 6 and 7. Although some important French studies are now available in translation, much of the new information is not easily accessible to English-speaking students, who are, as Ellis points out, largely 'isolated therefore from the mainstream of current Napoleonic research abroad'. Because of this, he continues, 'Our knowledge and understanding of Napoleon's impact on France and on Europe remains old-fashioned, lop-sided and is now increasingly mistaken. So far from coming up with fresh answers we appear not even to be asking the sort of questions which historians across the Channel have been doing for some thirty years'. This is an important point, for while significant contributions have been made by English-speaking historians in the last few decades to the study of the Ancien Régime and the Revolution they have made little impact on Napoleonic studies. Students and the general reader still have to rely heavily on traditional textbooks which take no account of recent research. Ellis himself in *The Napoleonic Empire* (1991) has begun to remedy this situation by providing a useful resumé of current European research on the effect of Napoleon's activities on France and Europe.

[*Note*: Strictly speaking, Napoleon should, prior to becoming Emperor in 1804, be referred to simply as Bonaparte, or General Bonaparte. It was not until 1802 that his full name appeared for the first time in official documents, when it was given as 'Napoleone Bonaparte'. (He had much earlier abandoned the Italian spelling of his surname, Buonaparte). Soon after 1802 the Italian version of his baptismal name was also dropped, in favour of the French, Napoléon. It was to be a source of conflict with his British gaolers on St Helena that, having been deprived by the Allies of his imperial title at the

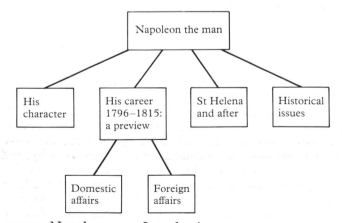

*Summary – Napoleon – an Introduction*

time of his second abdication in 1815, they addressed their prisoner as 'General Bonaparte'. The argument continued even after his death in a very undignified way. The British officials on the island would not agree to the name 'Napoléon' being put on the coffin, and as the French representatives there would accept nothing else, he was buried anonymously.

For the sake of simplicity, Napoleon, the anglicised form of his name, is used throughout this book.]

## Making notes on 'Napoleon – an Introduction'

This chapter is by way of being a 'scene-setter'. It is not likely, therefore, that you will need to make detailed notes on its contents. More important is that you should begin to understand something about Napoleon himself – what sort of person he was. Write down very briefly your present impression of him and his abilities. You will be able to add to this 'pen-portrait' as you read on.

Napoleon's personality is an extremely difficult one to interpret and the situation is further complicated by the fact that much of what he said about himself was contradictory. His habit of lying, consciously or otherwise, about himself and his motives makes it even more difficult than is usually the case with a public figure to determine the truth about him and the events with which he was involved.

You may find that your initial views on his character alter as you work through this book and perhaps go on to read some of the books suggested for further study (see page 144). Whatever conclusions you finally reach, whether you end up liking or loathing him, it is unlikely that you will remain indifferent to him.

## Answering essay questions on 'Napoleon, France and Europe'

The majority of examination questions on Napoleon fall, quite straightforwardly, under one of two main headings: his domestic policy (how he gained power and how he maintained it) *or* his imperial adventure (how and why he was able conquer most of Europe so easily, and how and why he was finally defeated). Such questions are usually quite specific, needing an amount of detailed knowledge to answer them, but they are also usually phrased in a straightforward manner, often beginning with how? or what? or why? In these cases, there is little difficulty in deciding what the examiner is asking you to do, as the examples discussed at the end of chapters 3, 4, 5, 6, and 7 illustrate. The difficulty lies in avoiding a dull, narrative answer.

Other, more open-ended questions on Napoleon also occur. These are mainly concerned with *relationships*. The relationship, for instance, between Napoleon and the Revolution (did he continue its achievements or destroy them?), or between Napoleon and France (did his rule benefit France or not?), or Napoleon and the countries of the Empire (were the effects of his rule to encourage nationalism?). Questions of this kind may be worded in a rather daunting manner, often based on a quotation for discussion ('challenging statement' questions). The answers certainly need a good deal of thought and careful planning, but, generally speaking, require less detailed factual knowledge than 'how?', 'what?' or 'why?' questions.

The most important thing is to make sure that you understand what any question is about, and that you know what you want to say – before you begin to write. Examples of open-ended questions of various kinds will be found at the end of most of the following chapters, while at the end of chapter 8 are some examples of very broad-based, general questions covering the whole topic of Napoleon, France and the Empire. These latter are superficially attractive, but are full of pit-falls and are often unexpectedly difficult to answer well.

# CHAPTER 2

# Brumaire

## 1 The Political Background to the *Coup d'État* of Brumaire

The early extremism of Revolutionary politics in France had come to an end by 1795, in which year a new and more moderate Constitution was adopted. Under it the government was headed by an executive of five Directors, but with only limited powers – they had no control over legislation for instance, for this was the prerogative of two councils. The first of these councils, the Five Hundred, could initiate legislation but not vote on it. They could then send it on for consideration to the second council known as the Ancients (250 men all aged at least 40) who could not discuss it, but only accept or reject it. These arrangements, intended to prevent dictatorship, meant that there was no single person or body in overall control of events and led to a series of political conflicts and stalemates. The Directors could not insist that the Councils pass a particular law nor veto any laws which they did pass. They could not dissolve the Councils, and the arrangements for altering the Constitution to enable them to do so were so time consuming that it would take nine years for any change to come into legal effect. The Directors, whose powers included control of the army, began to use force to interfere unconstitutionally with the composition of the Councils in the hope of making them more compliant. In 1797 the army was used in a *coup* expelling the newly elected royalist majority among the deputies, and in 1798 the Directors, with military support, annulled that year's elections because they produced a Jacobin (extreme revolutionary) majority. In 1799 the Directors decided to make use of the army again and began looking for a popular and successful general who could organise the military support they needed to force through changes in the constitution, and who would be willing to retire gracefully from political life afterwards. Although he was not their first or even second choice, they eventually settled on Napoleon as a suitable candidate. The result, though, was not to be what they expected – or wanted.

## 2 The *Coup d'État* Itself

The circumstances leading to the *coup* itself are not entirely clear, for accounts are confused and contradictory. However, what is clear is that in the summer of 1799 Napoleon, then campaigning in Egypt (see page 21), read in some old English newspapers of French defeats in Europe. Not knowing that the Directory had in fact already ordered his recall to France, he took the law into his own hands and abandoned the army to his second-in-command, declaring that 'The circumstances in which

France is placed have made it my imperative duty to return there'.

He landed safely on the south coast of France in early October and made his way to Paris where he was welcomed with enthusiasm by crowds who gathered everywhere he went. The civilian population knew of his past victories in Italy and Egypt and greeted him as a hero, while the army hailed him as the leader needed to overthrow a weak government of which they were tired and which was losing touch with its Revolutionary roots. He wrote later of his triumphal journey to Paris:

> 1 The joy was universal. It was not like the return of a citizen to his
>   country or a general at the head of a victorious army, but like the
>   triumph of a sovereign restored to his people. The people seemed
>   to say, We want a leader to direct us; we now behold him and our
> 5 glory will once more shine forth. I was . . . resolved to possess
>   myself of authority and to restore France to her former glory. Let
>   the deliverer give proof of his existence and the nation instinctive-
>   ly acknowledges and calls on him; all obstacles vanish at his
>   approach and a great people thronging round his steps seems,
> 10 exultingly, to proclaim 'This is the man!'.

Once in Paris Napoleon had a series of secret meetings with Sieyès, one of the Directors, who was dissatisfied with the existing Constitution. By early November detailed preparations were complete for a *coup* to bring a new Constitution into operation. A meeting of the Council of Ancients was to be called for early in the morning of 9 November at which the members would be 'persuaded' that that there was a plot by anarchists and foreigners to destroy the Republic. They would then agree that the government's only safety lay in moving themselves and the Council of the Five Hundred out of Paris into the suburbs, and in putting Napoleon in command of the Paris garrison of some 8000 troops and the government defence force of 1500 grenadiers. He would then be able to 'take all measures necessary for the safety of the nation's representatives', who 'in the shelter of his protecting arms may discuss peacefully the changes which the public interest renders necessary'.

The Ancients met as arranged and, after agreeing to the move from Paris, summoned Napoleon before them to swear a prepared oath of loyalty to the government. When he arrived at the council chamber, he made a speech instead, concluding with the words, 'What we want is a republic founded on true liberty, civil liberty and national representation; and we are going to have it. I swear it, in my name and in that of my comrades in arms'. Despite not being exactly what they had asked for, the Ancients accepted these words and allowed Napoleon to leave. Once outside the building he harangued his troops in much the same words as he had used to the Ancients and issued an Order of the Day expressing his belief that the army would support him 'with the energy, steadfastness and confidence' which he had always found in it before.

The following day, 10 November, after considerable delays in finding suitable furnishings for the makeshift council chambers hastily prepared in the palace of St Cloud on the outskirts of Paris, the Ancients and the Five Hundred began their deliberations just after noon. News soon reached them that all the Directors had either resigned or were under arrest, and that, without an executive, the Directory was, therefore, at an end. The way was open for the deputies to set up a new, provisional government. As the meetings of the two Councils continued without any decisions being reached, Napoleon, waiting in an outer room, became impatient. Without warning, and uninvited, he burst into the Council of the Ancients and began to speak.

Exactly what happened next is disputed. Napoleon's secretary, a hostile witness, declared that 'he made no speech to the Ancients unless a conversation held without nobility and without dignity can be called a speech. Only a few words could be heard, 'brothers-in-arms', 'plain-speaking of a soldier' . . . repeating several times 'That is all I have to say to you' – and he was saying nothing'. The official version of the speech, probably provided by Napoleon himself, and published the following day, was very different. Far from the 'incoherent babbling' usually attributed to him on this occasion by historians, he was represented as delivering a reasoned and statesmanlike account of his part in events to date. He denied that he was an intriguer or a political opportunist, urged the Ancients 'to act in saving liberty, saving equality', and promised that when this was done he would act as 'nothing more than the arm to support what you have established'. The report continued:

1  Yesterday I was staying quietly in Paris, when I was summoned by you to provide military support for the transfer to St Cloud. Now I am attacked as a new Caesar . . . and there is talk of a military government. But I am only acting through and for you.
5  The Republic has abdicated – the Directors have resigned or are under police protection – the Five Hundred is at sixes and sevens. Everything depends on the Ancients . . . I am not an intriguer: you know me well enough for that: I think I have given sufficient pledges of my devotion to my country. If I am a traitor it is for
10  each of you to be a Brutus. But if anyone calls for my outlawry, then the thunderbolt of war shall crush him. Remember that I march hand in hand with the god of fortune and of war!

As it is known that public speaking was never his strong point, the printed report probably represents what he afterwards wished he had said, rather than what he actually did say.

Leaving the Ancients to continue their debate, Napoleon, accompanied by four grenadiers, went on to where a stormy meeting of the Five

Hundred was being held. The Jacobin majority was arguing fiercely against a proposal that the Directory should be replaced by a stronger executive body, when Napoleon entered the room. Again it is not clear exactly what happened, for there are once more a number of conflicting accounts. However, it seems that many of the Five Hundred suspected Napoleon of plotting to make himself military ruler of France under a new constitution forced through the Councils with the help of the army, for he was immediately greeted with cries of 'Outlaw the dictator'. This was a dangerous development, for if a decree of outlawry were agreed, it would mean summary execution by a firing squad.

*Napoleon and the Council of Five Hundred at St Cloud by Bouchot*

   The recently appointed president of the Five Hundred, Napoleon's brother Lucien Bonaparte, was unable to quell the disorder which immediately broke out in the chamber, or to prevent the demand that a debate be held on the proposed outlawry. Meanwhile, after being much jostled and roughly handled by some of the deputies, Napoleon was rescued by the four grenadiers who managed to escort him to safety outside in the courtyard where other soldiers were waiting. Once there, pale and shaken, near fainting and incapable of action, he could only say 'I simply went to inform the deputies of the means of saving the republic, but they answered me with dagger-blows', pointing to his face which had a slight smear of blood, probably made accidentally by his own finger nails. This theme of the daggers was quickly taken up by Lucien who had hurried from the Council to join his brother:

1 The president declares that the vast majority of the Council is for the moment living in terror of several representatives with stilettos . . . confronting their colleagues with the most dreadful threats. These brigands are no longer representatives of the 5 people, but of the dagger. The Five Hundred is dissolved.

Lucien then staged a dramatic scene for the benefit of the waiting troops. After denouncing 'the minority of assassins' among the deputies, he drew his sword, and swore to kill his brother with it if Napoleon ever threatened the liberty of the French people. He then called on the army to follow their general and 'employ force against these disturbers'. Napoleon, now recovered from his fright, ordered the soldiers to advance against the Five Hundred. Led by an officer shouting 'Kick them all out', the men marched with fixed bayonets, and to the sound of a drum the Five Hundred were driven out of the room in less than five minutes, many of them escaping through the windows.

When the Ancients heard what had happened, they quickly agreed to the formal abolition of the Directory, the creation of a three-man executive, and the replacement of the two legislative Councils by two provisional Standing Committees of 25 members each.

By evening 'the agitators, intimidated, had dispersed and gone away' while 'others [of the Five Hundred] protected now from the [dagger] blows, came freely back to the Council room, and propositions necessary to the safety of the public were heard'. Under the chairmanship of the indefatigable Lucien, 'The salutary resolution which is to become the new and provisional law of the republic was discussed and prepared' by a rump of a hundred or so deputies. This 'Law of Brumaire', in addition to accepting the proposals of the Ancients, named as the three provisional consuls Sieyès, the non-entity Ducos (another former Director), and Napoleon.

The *coup* was over. The Napoleonic era was about to begin.

*A contemporary British cartoon depicting Napoleon as a crowned crocodile*

## 3 Why was the *Coup* Successful?

The nineteenth-century French historian de Toqueville wrote of Brumaire that it was 'One of the worst conceived and worst conducted *coups* imaginable, which succeeded only by virtue of the all powerful nature of its causes – the state of mind of the public and the disposition of the army'. Was de Toqueville right in this judgement?

The *coup* certainly was beset by confusion, both in its organisation and in its execution. While Sieyès and Napoleon seemed to be in agreement beforehand on their political aims, this accord was more apparent than real. Sieyès said afterwards that he had intended Napoleon to destroy the Directory and then quietly withdraw, leaving the field clear for Sieyès himself to take control at the head of a new executive. Napoleon later admitted that in the days before the *coup*, he promised that Sieyès' own 'wordy constitution would be put into effect'. It seems unlikely that he made such a promise without being offered something in return; but he never admitted it.

Most historians credit Sieyès with wanting a *coup* which would bring about change by peaceful means, and strengthen the executive without disturbing the political equilibrium. Events on 18 Brumaire went in accordance with his plans and represent the first act of the *coup*, with Sieyès in charge. There was no public reaction and all was quiet in the capital that night. Sieyès was confident that the Councils would agree to his proposals in the morning but delays in starting the meetings gave the opposition party in the Five Hundred time to muster their objections to changes in the constitution. This, combined with Napoleon's impatience for action, changed the whole nature of the *coup* and marked the beginning of its second act, with Napoleon in charge. Did Napoleon intend all along to seize control of events? It seems probable that he did. His triumphal progress through France on his return from Egypt, his speeches at the time, and his later assertion that, during the weeks of discussion before the *coup*, he was always following 'the interest of his own plans', all suggest it.

What about de Tocqueville's assertion that 'the state of mind of the public' was a prime cause of the *coup*'s success? Is there any evidence of a popular demand for a change of government? Or did it come about by default?

Opinions are divided about the state of France at the end of 1799. It was long fashionable among historians to accept unquestioningly that at the time France was socially and economically at a very low ebb. Roads were like 'ploughed fields', travel was dangerous because of robbers and worse, everywhere there was poverty and depravity resulting from a widespread decline in trade and industry and a break down of law and order. With royalist risings in the west causing civil war at home and the armies of the Second Coalition (Britain, Russia, Austria and the Ottoman Empire) threatening an invasion of France, there was defeatist talk of a Bourbon restoration and an accompanying fear that the achievements of the Revolution would be destroyed. This ultra gloomy picture is now largely discredited for it is known to have been based on reports sent in to Napoleon by his newly-appointed officials in the provinces. *The Great Survey of Year IX* and numerous pamphlets, such as *The State of France at the end of Year VIII*, constituted a determined government effort to blacken the record of the Directory and justify the *coup d'état*, to the advantage of the officials and of Napoleon himself. It is an early example of the Napoleonic propaganda machine at work.

While it would be equally wrong to suggest that all was entirely well with France in 1799, recent research has shown that the Directory, faced with serious problems beyond its immediate control, coped with them much better than had previously been thought. As well as making great efforts to improve the country's administrative and financial systems, it managed in a period of general economic depression to maintain and in some areas even increase French prosperity by the end of 1799. It was to be Napoleon's good fortune that a general upturn in the economy coincided with his coming to power and lasted for several years.

In other ways, too, the Directory achieved more than its successors were prepared to acknowledge. A royalist revolt was contained in south-west France and the armies of the Directory managed several, if rather minor, victories abroad against their enemies of the Second Coalition. The prospect was not entirely bleak in 1799, and most historians would now disagree with the old argument that the ease with which Napoleon seized power was due solely to the French people's 'need for a saviour' to bring order out of chaos and to restore law and order. The French historian Tulard is something of an exception here. He believes that Napoleon was the archetype and founding member of a long line of 'saviours, culminating in de Gaulle, and forming the chief landmarks in the history of nineteenth and twentieth century France'. In his opinion Napoleon was the 'saviour' needed by France. His mission was to preserve the security of recently acquired property (*biens nationaux*) and its owners, and to bring the Revolution to an end while maintaining its gains and stabilising its achievements. Disaster overtook him when he departed from this brief and involved France in the imperial adventure.

What evidence is there that the property-owning classes supported Napoleon at the time of the *coup*? Property owners included large landowners and wealthy urban middle-class citizens (the bourgeoisie) who had bought up the *biens nationaux* (royalist and church lands seized by the state early in the Revolution and sold off to anyone able to pay), as well as small farmers and even a few peasants. These two latter groups, freed by the Revolution from payment of tithes and feudal dues, had in some cases been able to buy small quantities of land. By 1795 when the Directory came to power, the constitution already embodied the ownership of private property as one of the rights sanctified by the Revolution. Although recent research has failed to find any evidence of clearly definable political views among the property-owning classes as a whole, many historians consider that the new property owners, especially the bourgeoisie, feared that a Jacobin revival or a Bourbon restoration would result in a government seizure of their recent acquisitions. Either of these events might occur, they believed, under the weak government of the Directory. They welcomed, therefore, the chance of strong government offered by the return of Napoleon, who seemed likely to protect them against Jacobins and Royalists alike.

Marxist historians argue that the property owning classes as a whole supported Napoleon because they were driven to it, whether they realised it or not, by the economic interests of the bourgeoisie. Industry and commerce needed foreign markets in order to expand. To obtain these markets would probably mean war, at least with Britain, and businessmen did not believe that the Directory would be able to win such a war. Only Napoleon, the general with the untarnished war record, could, in their view, reasonably be expected to do so.

In fact, Napoleon's seizure of power does not seem initially to have aroused much public interest or enthusiasm in any class of society, property-owning or otherwise. What historians have called a 'cloud of political apathy' had settled down heavily on France under the Directory, after the great upheavals of the early Revolution. It even became difficult in the late 1790s to persuade candidates to come forward for election as local officials. When the *coup* came there was little or no political reaction, probably because it appeared at first to most people to be just another of the Directory's temporary manoeuvres – a mere cosmetic substitution of consuls for directors. Not until Napoleon's policies became clear (see page 83) did the property-owners rally to his side and his interests become theirs.

What about de Toqueville's 'disposition of the army' as a factor in the *coup*? By 1799 the use of the army in civilian politics had become an accepted fact – the Directory had called on them successfully in 1797 and 1798 to maintain itself in power – but in 1799 the situation was different. The Directors realised too late that they had lost control of events when they put the Paris garrison of 8000 or so regular troops under Napoleon's command, especially when they failed to extract from him the very specific oath of loyalty they had at first demanded. The soldiers knew Napoleon as the General who had arranged for the Army of Italy to receive half their wages in cash, not in depreciated paper money, a decision which had made him personally enormously popular, even before he won a single victory. With the glory of his Italian and Egyptian campaigns still upon him, they were well disposed to do whatever he ordered, particularly after he promised on 19 Brumaire to remedy their grievances against the government. These were mainly concerned with holes in their shoes, a shortage of tobacco and delays in payment of their wages. The *coup* could not have been carried out successfully without the intimidating presence of the army at St Cloud, nor without its help in dispersing the opposition members of the Five Hundred.

There was one other small, but highly important, group of supporters of the *coup* who were extremely influential in ensuring its success. These supporters were to be found among the Ancients and the Five Hundred. Research suggests that in the weeks before the *coup* the conspirators worked hard on the deputies, and by various means, mostly financial, bought the allegiance of many of them. A great number of the Ancients were apparently given advance information on the *coup* and agreed to support it, for no difficulty of any kind was raised about moving the Councils to St Cloud, thus enabling the *coup* to take place. Even more significant was the election, immediately prior to the *coup*, of Napoleon's brother, Lucien, to be President of the Five Hundred, where he acted as a counter-balance to the Jacobin majority. His presence there proved invaluable and his role in the later stages of the *coup* was crucial to its success. Without his decisive action, his brother's bid for power would have ended prematurely, almost certainly in death, shot as an outlaw.

The whole *coup* had been a muddled affair, and had been lucky to succeed at all. If there were a hero, it was Lucien; Napoleon emerged as hesitant and indecisive, and with little credit. These facts, though, were speedily disguised by Napoleonic propaganda, and Lucien – after a short spell as Minister of the Interior when he made himself useful to his brother in manipulating the results of the first plebiscite – was removed from the government and sent out of the limelight into near exile as ambassador to Spain.

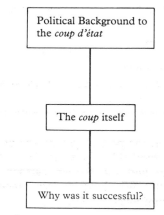

Political Background to the *coup d'état*

The *coup* itself

Why was it successful?

*Summary – Brumaire*

*Making Notes on 'Brumaire'*

Again, this is a chapter on which detailed notes are unnecessary for examination purposes. Instead use the information you now have to write down briefly the points needed to answer the following questions:
1 What were the *main* events of the *coup*?
2 Why was it successful? Was the success deserved?
3 What light do the events of November 1799 throw on Napoleon's character and ability?

*Answering source-based questions on 'Brumaire'*

**1 Napoleon and the *Coup***
Read the short extracts on pages 10 and 11 and answer the following questions:
a) In the extract on page 10, how does Napoleon see himself? How does he see the people? (*6 marks*)
b) Bearing in mind that this account was written some years after the event, is it likely to reflect accurately Napoleon's opinions at the time? If this is not the case, what was his purpose in writing it? (*2 marks*)
c) In Napoleon's speech to the Council (page 11) explain briefly what were i) 'the Ancients', and ii) the 'Five Hundred'. Also explain the references to iii) 'Caesar' and 'Brutus', and to iv) 'outlawry'. What did Napoleon mean by v) 'The Republic has abdicated'? (*5 marks*)
d) In the light of the threat contained in the final sentences (lines 11–12) what is Napoleon's message to the Council? (*2 marks*)

**2 Two versions of Brumaire**
Look carefully at the painting and cartoon on pages 12 and 14 and answer the following questions:
a) Describe the way in which Napoleon is portrayed in the painting. How has the artist achieved his effect? Is the overall impression favourable or unfavourable to Napoleon? Explain your answer. (*6 marks*)
b) In the cartoon, explain the part played by the choice of animals in achieving the effect intended by the artist. (*5 marks*)
c) The French painting and the British cartoon served a similar purpose. What was it? Which of the two pictures is the more successful? Explain your answer. (*4 marks*)

# CHAPTER 3

# Napoleon and Europe – Victory and Defeat: The Main Events

## 1 The Road to Victory

a) The Early Campaigns – Italy and Egypt 1796–9

It was the Italian campaigns of 1796–7 with a dozen victories in less than a year which made Napoleon's name as a general. They not only set the seal on his military reputation, but provided the starting point for the Legend (see page 123). As a result, much of what has been written about the campaigns, by Napoleon and others, is a fanciful embellishment of the facts. The often repeated account of how a young, insignificant general who was very much a political appointee dramatically won over to his side the sceptical veteran officers of the Army of Italy is a considerable exaggeration. Napoleon was already well known to the officers concerned, who, far from deriding him, seem to have welcomed him on his arrival as the man most likely to lead them to victory. There is no official record of the rousing piece of oratory which he is alleged to have delivered as his first speech to the army, and which appears in the St Helena account. Instead of the colourful promises of 'rich provinces and great cities which will be in your power' together with 'honour and glory when I lead you into the most fertile plains in the world', there was in reality only a rather staid and mundane order of the day. The army itself is commonly described as dispirited and demoralised, so making Napoleon's achievement in bringing it speedily up to scratch appear all the greater. In fact, although the army had not had much success since 1792 and was badly clothed and fed (mainly because of corrupt administration), it consisted of experienced and hardened campaigners, mostly volunteers or regulars, and its discipline and morale were generally good. All it needed was inspiring leadership, and this Napoleon provided.

Within a month of his arrival in Italy he had conquered and occupied Piedmont, and at the beginning of May 1796 was crossing the River Po in pursuit of the Austrian army into Lombardy. He seems to have regarded the subsequent battle of Lodi and the entry into Milan as a psycholgical turning point in his career, giving him the confidence that he could 'perform great things, which hitherto had been only a fantastic dream'. Italy lay wide open to the plundering French soldiers as they marched south defeating four separate Austrian armies as they went. In February 1797 with the capture of Mantua the French conquest of northern Italy was complete.

Napoleon next moved against Austria itself and a month later was only just over 60 miles from Vienna where, with his army exhausted and dangerously far from base, he offered the Austrians preliminary peace terms. While these terms were awaiting ratification, Napoleon completed his triumphant Italian campaign by occupying the Republic of Genoa (which adopted a French-style constitution and became the Ligurian Republic), by overrunning part of the Republic of Venice and by concluding on his own initiative an agreement with the Pope. He then installed himself and his wife Josephine in near-royal splendour in a castle near Milan.

The Treaty of Campo Formio (October 1797), negotiated by Napoleon, consolidated French gains into the newly formed Cisalpine Republic (Modena, Ferrara, Reggio, Bolgna and the Romagna, with the addition of Lombardy and the former Venetian possessions of the Ionian islands and part of Dalmatia). This vassal state was given a system of government based on the French constitution of 1795 and its executive and legislative bodies were nominated by Napoleon himself. 'Only he can make peace, and he can do it on any terms he wants' was the comment of one Austrian envoy in Paris. It seemed a brilliant peace from the point of view of French national prestige and was received as such in Paris where Napoleon was given a hero's welcome.

The need to keep this potentially dangerous young man and his unemployed troops busy and out of politics, led the Directory to send him with the Army of the Orient to invade Egypt. Despite the early loss of his fleet, destroyed by Nelson in Aboukir Bay in July 1798, which cut the 'Army of the Orient' off from France, Napoleon again distinguished himself in the field at the battle of the Pyramids. Egypt was quickly occupied but an advance into Syria was ultimately less successful. Napoleon, overconfident after capturing Jaffa, blundered badly at the siege of Acre. After losing half his men, he gave up the attempt to capture the fortress and returned to Egypt. There he received news which sent him hurrying back to France in August 1799 (see page 9). (The army, thus unceremoniously abandoned, managed somehow to survive without him until its final defeat in 1801 by a British expeditionary force).

## i) Assessment

The campaigns in Italy and to a lesser extent in Egypt were a foretaste of what was to come. Militarily, they showed Napoleon at his best, and are a model for the later blitzkrieg strategies which he used so successfully to win battle after battle against the old-fashioned and disunited armies of the enemy until 1808 (see pages 39–41). They are illuminating in other ways too, for they show that many of the personality traits which came to be associated with Napoleon were already well established – among them, great personal ambition, supreme self-confidence, determination and ruthlessness, as well as undisputed powers of leadership. He frequently exceeded his orders,

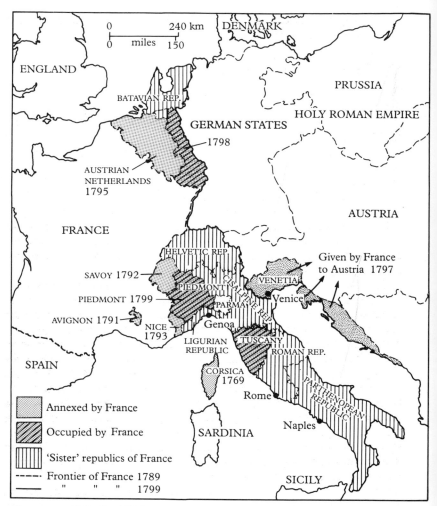

*France and Italy 1799*

however, particularly in the matter of negotiating terms, and could be guilty of unnecessary cruelty, ordering the coldblooded murder of 3000 prisoners after the fall of Jaffa, for instance.

The 150 scholars and scientific experts who accompanied him to Egypt did excellent work, but his motives for taking them are not entirely clear. He may have been genuinely interested, especially as he had just been made a member of the *Institut de France*, and it is true that Egyptian influence was later to feature in the Empire style of furniture and interior decoration, but his propaganda at the time suggests, rather, that he was already thinking of himself as a modern day

Alexander or Julius Caesar, combining military success with learning in the course of founding a new empire.

## b)  Wars of the Consulate and Early Empire 1800–7

The need for an early victory and a quick peace after the *coup d'état* of November 1799 in order to strengthen his own position as First Consul led Napoleon back to Italy. There in June 1800, after a march across the Alps, he inflicted a decisive defeat on the Austrians at Marengo. A further French victory at Hohenlinden in Bavaria six months later brought about the peace of Lunéville. It recognised French possession of Belgium (the Austrian Netherlands) as well as the left bank of the Rhine and the gains in Italy. Austria lost control of all northern Italy, except Venetia, and her influence in Germany was reduced. With the collapse of the Second Coalition (see page 45) Britain agreed to the Peace of Amiens (March 1802) by which France withdrew from the Papal States and Naples, and Britain returned most of her conquests, including Egypt which was restored to the Ottoman Empire.

The peace settlement proved an unstable one, a mere truce in a war which had already been going on for almost a decade. After a period of increasingly acrimonious relations between France and Britain over breaches of the spirit if not the letter of the peace treaty on both sides, war broke out again in May 1803. Mastery on land lay with France, dominance at sea with Britain. Neither in itself was sufficient for victory. Napoleon tried to remedy this at the end of 1803 by the assembly of a fleet and a vast army at Boulogne. There for the next two years both remained poised for an invasion of England. The invasion plans came to nothing, mainly because Napoleon would not admit that his knowledge of naval matters was rudimentary. He had no understanding of the sea or its ways, nor of the importance of wind and weather in the deployment of sailing ships. By insisting, for instance, against all advice that the fleet put to sea for a review on a day when a storm was brewing, he caused great disorder and damage among the ships when the 'great tempest blew and dispersed them, so that they were like to be destroyed'. His whole plan for the invasion was unsound, depending not only on suitable weather conditions, but also on the unlikely event of effecting at the same time a French command of the sea for long enough to transport the army across the Channel. The idea had to be abandoned in October 1805 when Nelson's victory at Trafalgar destroyed the combined Franco-Spanish fleet, needed to lure the British ships away from the Channel, before it could reach the scene of operations. Even before this French disaster, Napoleon had gathered up his Army of England and marched south to the Danube to confront Austria, which had declared war on France during the summer.

* The campaigns of 1805–7 which followed Napoleon's departure

from Boulogne showed him at his military best, winning a series of crushing victories against the armies of Austria, Prussia and Russia. The latest incompetent Austrian general was outmanoeuvred and forced to surrender at Ulm in October 1805. The defeat of an Austro-Russian army at Austerlitz in December caused Russia to retreat rapidly out of Napoleon's reach and Austria to agree to the treaty of Pressburg, which recognised French supremacy in northern Italy and the loss of Austrian authority in Germany. Complicated negotiations between Napoleon and Prussia involving Prussia's acquisition of Hanover in return for adherence to Napoleon's Continental Blockade (see page 47) led to a breakdown of relations and then to war between the two countries. In a remarkable one-week campaign Napoleon destroyed Prussia at the twin battles of Jena-Auerstädt (October 1806). In February 1807 Napoleon marched through Poland to attack Russia, his remaining continental enemy, winning a technical victory over the Russians in the bitter battle of Eylau. A major defeat at Friedland in June convinced the Russians of the need to make peace. This was done in July 1807 at Tilsit in a personal meeting between Napoleon and Tsar Alexander I. This took place initially (it was continued on dry land) on a raft in the middle of the River Niemen, which marked the Russian frontier.

## i) Assessment

In two years (1805–7) and a series of short campaigns, Napoleon had in turn defeated three of his four opponents. In November 1806 he established the Continental Blockade to deal with the remaining one, Britain, who had taken no active part in the war, restricting herself to supplying her allies with subsidies. His achievements were truly astounding. He had established French dominance in Germany by defeating Austria, abolishing the Holy Roman Empire and replacing it with the French satellite state of the Confederation of the Rhine. He had destroyed Prussian power, converted Prussian Poland into the Grand Duchy of Warsaw as a barrier against Russia, and Prussia's west German lands into the new satellite kingdom of Westphalia. In Italy he had crowned himself King of Italy, had added Parma and Tuscany to the existing French possessions of Piedmont and Lombardy, and made Naples into another satellite. In the east he had not only forced Russia to make peace in 1807, but had won Tsar Alexander over to a formal alliance with France, so protecting his Empire from an attack on its eastern boundaries. By the end of the year Napoleon controlled directly or indirectly the greater part of Europe. The 'Grand Empire' had come into being, but the seeds of its destruction were already sown, for in 1807 had also begun the Spanish adventure (see page 25).

## 2  Road to Defeat 1808–14

In one of his last successful military forays, at the beginning of 1808, Napoleon invaded and occupied the Papal States in furtherance of his demand that the Pope should enforce the Continental Blockade:

> 1 His Holiness is sovereign of Rome, but I am the Emperor. My enemies must be his enemies. When Charlemagne made the popes temporal sovereigns he meant them to remain vassals of the [Holy Roman] Empire; nowadays. Far from regarding themselves
> 5 as vassals of the Empire, they refuse to belong to it at all . . . In the circumstances the only possible course was to occupy Rome with troops . . . and to reduce the popes to their proper rank . . .

The acquisition of the Papal States consolidated Napoleon's hold over Italy, all of which, apart from the island of Sicily, was now French.

Although the Empire continued to grow until 1811, a decline in Napoleon's fortunes is clear from 1808 onwards. Among the causes are his two great 'mistakes' – the Spanish and Russian campaigns. Both, like the invasion of the Papal States were brought about by his obsession with enforcing the Continental Blockade along the whole European coast line, from the Mediterranean to the White Sea. While British sea-power remained superior, Napoleon had no chance of defeating Britain by direct military means. The best he could hope for was to use his land-based power as an economic weapon by making use of his control over the European coastline to prevent British trade with Europe (see pages 63 and 113).

### a)  The Spanish Campaign

The Spanish campaign (more appropriately described as the Iberian or Peninsular war, for Portugal as well as Spain was involved) resulted in the eventual loss of about half of the 600,000 French soldiers who served there. It also failed totally in its primary objective, for despite the overrunning of Portugal in 1807, the Blockade became no more effective. The value of British exports entering Europe through Portuguese ports actually doubled between 1808 and 1809 to nearly a million pounds, and by 1811 the annual total had increased to more than six million.

Franco-Spanish relations had not been of the most amicable between 1799 and 1807 as Napoleon sought to impress on Spain that her position was simply that of a French ally whose duty was to supply men and money as required. When she failed to do so satisfactorily, Napoleon merely removed her king and his heir, and substituted a ruler of his own choice whom he could control, his brother Joseph. Joseph, previously the popular King of Naples, was gravely disappointed on

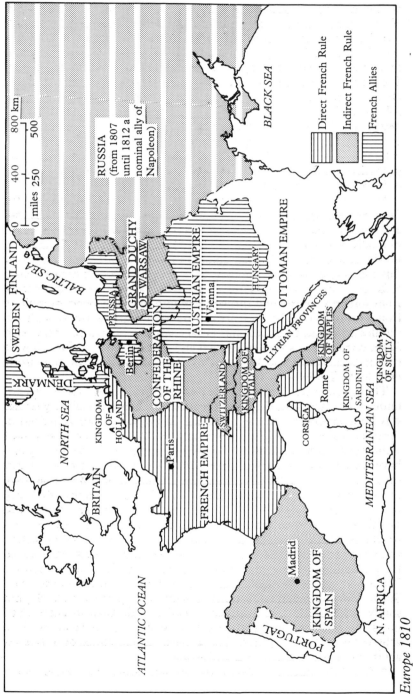

Europe 1810

arrival in Spain. 'Not a single Spaniard is on my side' he wrote, while Murat led an army to occupy Madrid and impose French rule. Murat's ferocious handling of a revolt by the people of Madrid in May 1808, the scenes immortalised by Goya's horrific paintings, roused the whole population to patriotic anger against the French occupying forces. Local resistance committees (*juntas*) were set up, co-ordinated by the clergy and members of the nobility, to raise guerilla fighters and regular soldiers and a small and comparatively inexperienced French army was defeated at Baylen by a mixed force of Spanish troops. The sensation created by this defeat brought Napoleon himself to Spain with 100,000 veterans of the *Grande Armée*. A British expeditionary force was despatched to the Peninsula in answer to a Spanish request for help and quickly drove the French out of Portugal.

Napoleon, distracted by news of Austrian mobilisation on the Danube, left Spain at the beginning of 1809. Without his leadership and with no other supreme commander, the war was left in the hands of mutually hostile generals. The aimiable Joseph did his best to pacify his unwilling subjects, with a fair amount of success, but in 1810 much of this conciliatory work was undone by Napoleon, who did not trust such softness. Without consultation, he removed large areas of the country from Joseph's control and turned them into semi-independent military frontier provinces. The presence of French and British troops added to the already existing political and social confusion of Spanish society and Spain remained in a state of turmoil and conflict until the French were driven back across the Pyrenees by Wellington in 1813 and finally defeated at Toulouse in 1814.

The Spanish war was never popular in France. It eroded French military prestige, and the long, inconclusive fighting against guerillas was both expensive and demoralising. If Napoleon had remained in Spain in January 1809 it is entirely arguable that he could have gained victory in a rapid campaign. He himself said afterwards that he ought to have stayed another month, have established his authority and taken the initiative. The delay in reaching the Danube which this would have caused would, it is true, have meant sacrificing gains there, and it may be that by 1809 Napoleon had decided that Spain was not worth such sacrifices. If so, then his mistake was leaving the army locked in a worthless conflict – was he too proud to withdraw them, admit failure and leave Spain to govern herself? – when he could so easily have solved the problem of how to stop British goods entering Europe through the Peninsula. All he needed to do was close his Pyrenees border with Spain. Difficult mountain country it might be to patrol effectively, but surely, with much of it impassable, easier to do than to guard 3000 miles of open coastline. He need never have invaded Spain at all to achieve his declared objective; but perhaps the temptation of adding yet another satellite to his list was irresistible.

*Elsewhere during 1809–11 the French army was doing rather

better. After leaving Spain, Napoleon reached the Danube valley in early March 1809, where he waited for the Austrians, whose army had been much strengthened since the defeats of 1805–6 and was now led by the extremely able Archduke Charles. (Wellington thought the Archduke the best general of the age. 'He knows more about it than all of us put together', he said). The campaign lasted just under two months. In April the Austrians were defeated at Eckmühl with severe losses, while in May, Napoleon, after successfully occupying Vienna, was equally heavily defeated at Aspern (Essling) and had to retire to a nearby island in the Danube. With honours even, a third encounter took place in mid-July at Wagram. It was the last of Napoleon's great victories. A pitched battle ended in an Austrian retreat and a request for an armistice. In October the Treaty of Schönbrunn was signed. It was a dictated peace in typical Napoleonic style. By it Austria lost the Illyrian provinces on the Adriatic coast, with their population of three and a half million, her army was reduced to 150,000 and she was forced to find nearly four million pounds indemnity. When the Austrian Emperor complained about the severity of the terms, Napoleon merely replied that if Austria had kept the peace made in 1801 at Lunéville, 'both countries might have been spared many sufferings'.

At the end of 1809 Napoleon decided to divorce Josephine and remarry in the hope of fathering an heir for the Empire (see page 82). Proposals for marriage with the Tsar's sister fell through, and the Austrian Emperor who 'will shrink from nothing that may contribute to the welfare and peace of the state' offered his daughter, Marie-Louise as a replacement. In March 1810, before the bride left for France, a proxy marriage took place in Vienna at which the bridegroom was represented by Napoleon's recent enemy, Archduke Charles! Austria and France might have officially become allies but the new Empress received only a lukewarm welcome in Paris. It was reported that the crowd which saw her arrive 'had been attracted only out of simple curiosity and showed neither enthusiasm nor joy'. She was after all the niece of Marie-Antoinette.

## b) The Russian Campaign 1812

The Franco-Russian *rapprochement* made at Tilsit was continued with difficulty on both sides until 1812. There were numerous causes of friction which arose largely because of mutual distrust. Each suspected the other of hostile expansionist aims in the Baltic, central Europe and the Balkans. Napoleon would not support the Tsar's ambitions to seize Istanbul – he had similar aspirations of his own. The Austrian marriage annoyed the Tsar, as did Napoleon's annexation of the North German coast and the Duchy of Oldenburg (the Tsar's sister was married to the Crown Duke) especially as the Duchy's independence had been guaranteed at Tilsit. With French encouragement the Tsar attacked

Sweden, but without French agreement seized and annexed Swedish Finland. There were arguments over the future of the Grand Duchy of Warsaw; but chiefly the disagreements arose over the Tsar's virtual withdrawal from the Continental Blockade. On the last day of 1810 he introduced a new trade tariff which discriminated against France and in favour of Britain. Napoleon determined on war to restore his dominance over the Tsar and to reinforce the Continental Blockade. During the next 12 months he built up the *Grande Armée* to more than 450,000 men (less than half of whom were French), plus 150,000 auxiliary troops and over 1000 guns.

In June 1812, without any declaration of war, Napoleon crossed the River Niemen. He was unable to use his usual strategy of luring the enemy towards him, and forcing a decisive battle early in the campaign. The much smaller Russian armies continually retreated before him, perhaps from strategic design, more probably because of rivalry and indecision in the Russian army. Either way, the result was to draw Napoleon ever deeper into Russia, extending his supply lines and increasing the difficulties for his large, slow-moving force which had no chance of catching up with the enemy. Medical supplies and food were short, and disease struck down 60,000 men even before the campaign had properly begun. Following in the scorched-earth wake of the Russian army, Napoleon found it difficult to feed his men – no living off the country here – and over 1000 cavalry horses died from eating unripe corn in the fields.

By the time Napoleon reached Vitebsk his army was so demoralised – it had already incurred the same number of casualties, either from disease or being picked off by skirmishing Cossacks, as would be expected from two large battles – the men had to rest for a fortnight. Pressing on to Smolensk they found the city had already been destroyed by the Russians and that no food or shelter was available there. The recently appointed Russian commander, the one-eyed Kutusov, urged on by the Tsar, now decided to stand and fight, and waited with an army of about 120,000 west of Moscow near the village of Borodino. There in a day-long battle on 7 September Napoleon won a technical victory after a prolonged artillery duel, but at great cost in men and guns. In his Order of the Day Napoleon, parodying Henry V at Agincourt, declared, 'Let them say this of you: He was present at this great battle under the walls of Moscow' (only the walls were still sixty miles away!). On 14 September Napoleon's advance guard rode into a deserted Moscow. The rest of the army followed, 'all clapping their hands and shouting, Moscow, Moscow'. Two days later, two-thirds of the city was in ruins, burnt down by fires started on orders of the Russian governor in order to destroy the food and ammunition left behind there.

The Tsar refused to negotiate despite the loss of Moscow. To do so would have been more than his life was worth – he would have been assassinated or deposed. Another Tilsit was impossible to contemplate in the patriotic fervour of the moment.

The unusually mild autumn tempted Napoleon to linger in Moscow for over a month. He ignored the warnings of bad weather to come, and only the eventual realisation that the *Grande Armée* would starve to death if he stayed longer in the ruined and empty city caused him to order a return home. Laden with loot and slowed down by their wounded, the army began the retreat on 19 October. Napoleon ordered them to take a route to the south of the one by which they had arrived, in the hope that there he would find in an unravaged countryside food and shelter for his men who now numbered only 107,000; but flank attacks by the waiting Russian army soon pushed the French north again and back onto their original route. This forced them to march over the battlefield of Borodino, still strewn with the stripped and decaying bodies of 30,000 of their own dead!

By the time Napoleon reached Smolensk in mid-November there were only 50,000 left in the *Grande Armée* itself. Sickness and skirmishers, famine and exhaustion had taken their toll, and the winter had only just begun to bite. In snow and intense cold the army, now further depleted, left Smolensk and marched west. The Russians reached the River Beresina (a tributary of the Niemen) before the French, and demolished the bridges. Thus prevented from escaping, Napoleon's army could be destroyed at the Russians' leisure. That anything of the *Grande Armée* and its auxiliary troops survived was due to Napoleon's discovery of a ford and the building of two emergency trestle bridges across the river in appalling conditions. In the panic struggle to reach safety, when the bridges were fired to prevent a Russian pursuit, thousands were drowned in the freezing water. Thousands more, together with the main mass of camp followers and their goods, were left behind on the bank to the mercy of the Russians. Of the 40,000 men of the *Grande Armée* who got safely across the bridges some 25,000 survived to reach Germany at the end of the year.

## i) Assessment

Despite the version of events put out by Napoleon in his famous 29th Bulletin, that it was the snow and ice, the intense cold and the frostbite which destroyed the *Grande Armée* this was not so. The army, together with its auxiliaries, was destroyed long before winter arrived in the first days of November. Twice as many men (35,000) were lost on the retreat in a week of fair weather in late October as were lost in a week of snow and ice on the road from Smolensk to the Beresina in mid-November. Even more instructive is the fact that 350,000 (more than half the total French forces) died *before* they reached Moscow. Napoleon lost his army by bad management, poor supply arrangements, lack of local knowledge, and over confidence. He had allowed himself nine weeks to defeat Russia and return in triumph to Germany. His army had only summer clothing and enough food for three weeks (he intended to be comfortably ensconced in Moscow as Emperor of the East by then). Many supplies proved inadequate or non-existent. There was no fodder for the horses nor frost nails for their shoes, no maps covering more than a few miles inside the Russian border, and no bandages for the wounded. There was unusual confusion in the French army command, too. General Caulincourt wrote after leaving Moscow, 'Never was a retreat worse planned, or carried out with less discipline; never did convoys march so badly ... To lack of forethought we owed a great part of our disaster'.

## c) The Last Campaigns 1813–15

Encouraged by the events of 1812, the Tsar masterminded the formation of a Fourth Coalition against Napoleon (see page 51) and an allied army advanced triumphantly across Europe in the early part of 1813. Napoleon, who had found difficulty in raising another army so soon, and in replacing the thousands of horses lost in Russia, decided after winning a technical victory over the allies at Bautzen in May to accept an armistice. This would, he hoped, give him a breathing space to build up his forces for a decisive campaign. Many historians consider this truce to have been a fatal mistake by Napoleon, for during it he lost his numerical military supremacy over the enemy when Austria, her military preparations complete, joined the allies (Russia, Prussia and England) in the Fourth Coalition. Final negotiations in Prague for a possible general peace treaty came to nothing – Napoleon would make no concessions, would surrender no territory. He could perhaps even at this late date have obtained peace on reasonable terms, retaining at least France's 'natural frontiers', and he might himself have continued as ruler of France. However, he seems to have feared that a negotiated settlement would mean the end of his power, for he was not one of the hereditary sovereigns of Europe. They, he said, could lose 20 battles and keep their thrones. He as an upstart soldier, could not. 'My domination will not survive the day when I cease to be strong and therefore feared'. War, rather than diplomacy, had always been his preference, and characteristically he chose to stake his all on military victory to settle the issue of his future.

Fighting resumed in August and, after two minor victories and a series of indecisive encounters, Napoleon's gamble finally failed at the Battle of the Nations at Leipzig (16–19 October). Outnumbered and outmanoeuvred, he was heavily defeated and forced back to the Rhine, his influence in Germany gone, the Grand Empire collapsing around him. One after another, Baden, Bavaria, Würtemberg and the other states of the Confederation went over to the Allies; Jérôme was driven out of Westphalia; Saxony fell into Prussian hands and the Grand Duchy of Warsaw into those of Russia. As the news of the battle spread

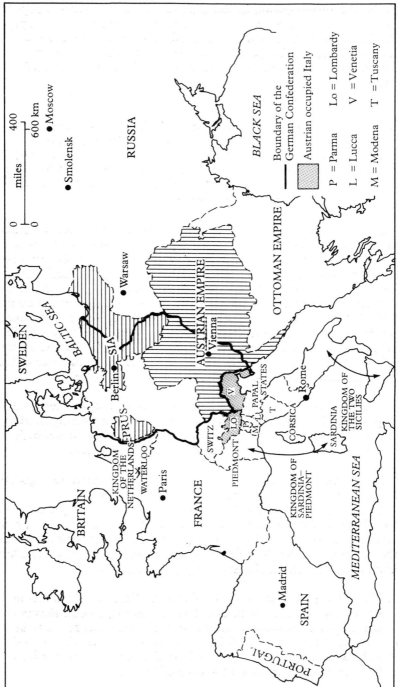

*Europe 1815*

so did the disintegration of the Empire. Within the week a popular
revolt in Amsterdam drove the French out of Holland; the Illyrian
Provinces had to be abandoned soon after; Spain was already lost, the
last of Napoleon's forces there streaming back into France and final
defeat. Only Belgium, Switzerland and Italy now constituted the
Empire.

One of his generals met Napoleon shortly after the battle:

1 He was sunk in gloom – with reason. Hardly two months had
  elapsed and an immense army of 400,000 men had melted away in
  his hands – for the second time in a year the world was presented
  with a spectacle of destruction . . . only about 60,000 men
5 remained. [When they reached the Rhine an outbreak of typhus
  killed about a third of these survivors.]

At home there was discontent and opposition as preparations began
in bitter winter weather for a new campaign. Napoleon set to work to
raise yet another army and to find the money to equip it. The financial
situation was desperate, the burden of conscription had become
intolerable in a country which had been 20 years at war, and despite the
fact that for the first time since 1792 France was facing invasion by the
'kings' of old Europe, reports made by the commissioners sent round
the provinces by Napoleon show that public morale was very low. The
people wanted peace; Napoleon wanted victory. He suspected the
Allies' motives in renewing the offer of a settlement on the basis of the
'natural frontiers', and demanded more. His envoy despaired:

  The Emperor did not see, or rather would not see, his true
  position. He deceived himself . . . about his own strength. He
  could not forget that he had once dictated to Europe, or reconcile
  himself to the idea of being dictated to in his own turn.

By the middle of January when Napoleon finally agreed to negotiate
it was too late. The Allied offer had been withdrawn.

In a campaign to defend the Rhine frontier in the early months of
1814 Napoleon won a number of small but impressive victories. These
successes, though, were not enough to stop the enemy advance, and at
the end of March the allies entered Paris. Napoleon's obstinacy had lost
him everything. He agreed, unwillingly, to abdicate:

1 The allied powers having proclaimed the Emperor Napoleon to
  be the sole obstacle to the re-establishment of peace in Europe,
  the Emperor Napoleon, faithful to his word, declares that he
  renounces for himself and his heirs the thrones of France and
5 Italy, and that there is no personal sacrifice, even life itself, which
  he is not ready to make for the good of France.

An attempt at suicide having failed – the poison, which he had carried round with him for emergency use on the Russian campaign, had been kept too long and had lost its potency – Napoleon took it as a sign for the future; 'Fate has decided that I must live and await all that Providence has in store for me. I abdicate and I yield nothing'.

Meanwhile, he accepted the generous offer of the Allies and retired, with his title of Emperor, to Elba in May 1814 while the future of France and her Empire was discussed at Vienna (see page 52). Ten months later Napoleon was back, proclaiming 'The eagle will fly from steeple to steeple until it reaches the towers of Notre Dame'. As *de facto* ruler of France again he hoped to become so by right by splitting the allies and recovering his throne. But Austria and Britain rejected his offers of separate negotiations, declared him an outlaw and aligned themselves with Prussia and Russia against him. He needed a quick military victory to unite France behind him and to reassert his authority over the country. On 14 June he issued what was to be his last Order of the Day: 'Soldiers . . . the Allies have begun the most unjust of aggressions. Let us march to meet them . . . for every Frenchman with a heart, the moment has come to conquer or perish'. He very nearly did conquer for Waterloo was a close fought battle. As Wellington said the next day 'it was a damned close thing – the nearest run thing you ever saw in your life'.

Undaunted, Napoleon at once began planning a new campaign: 'All is not lost. I suppose that when I reassemble my forces I shall have . . . 150,000 men ready immediately to bring against the enemy. I will use carriage horses to drag the guns, raise another 100,000 men by conscription, arm them with muskets taken from the royalists . . .'. It was not to be. 'We are not going to begin all over again' was the

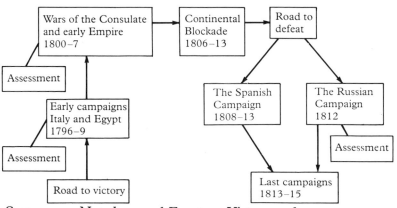

*Summary – Napoleon and Europe – Victory and Defeat : the Events*

comment by the Council of State. Without political or popular support Napoleon had no option but to agree to demands for his second abdication. His proposal that a Regency should be set up for Napoleon II, his young son, was ignored. On 8 July Louis XVIII made his second entry into Paris. The First Empire was finally at an end.

---

***Making notes on*** *'Napoleon and Europe – Victory and Defeat: The Events'*

This chapter is a straightforward, necessarily brief narrative account of Napoleon's activities in Europe 1796–1815 – a story of early victory and ultimate defeat. For most examination purposes, unless you hope to answer one of the *very* occasional questions set on specific campaigns, an outline knowledge of events is all that is required. The information contained in this chapter taken together with that in the Chronological Table on pages 140–1 will provide that outline. Having established the course of events, the next chapter looks at Napoleon's abilities as a military commander and the reasons *why* his success was followed by disaster.

CHAPTER 4

# Napoleon and Europe – Victory and Defeat: The Reasons Why

## 1 Napoleon Victorious 1800–7

Why was Napoleon able to achieve so easily almost complete control over Europe between 1800 and 1807? The reasons can best be considered under two main headings – his strengths, and his enemies' weaknesses.

### a) Napoleon's Strength – The Military Aspect

*i) Napoleon's Qualities of Leadership*
One of Napoleon's great strengths as leader was the devotion of his men. His soldiers adored him. Why was this?

Despite his generally unprepossessing appearance, when he wished to charm he could quickly win over anyone he met, however initially hostile they might be. Within a couple of days he had completely captivated the officers and crew of the *Bellerophon* taking him to St Helena in 1815, much alarming the British government. 'If he had obtained an interview with His Royal Highness the Prince Regent', exclaimed one Admiral at the time,'in half an hour they would have been the best friends in England!' His contemporaries had no doubt about the charismatic quality of his leadership. His great adversary Wellington said of him that the moral effect of his presence in the field was worth an additional force of 40,000 men to the French army. This he ascribed partly to Napoleon's dual position as both head of state and commander-in-chief (see below, pages 44–5) which gave him unparalleled control over events, but also to his great personal popularity with the army. One of Napoleon's own generals explained this popularity by saying that it 'was by familiarities that the Emperor made his soldiers adore him, but it was a means available only to a commander whom frequent victories had made illustrious; any other general would have injured his reputation by it'. Even the London *Times* in its obituary notice of July 1821 remarked that 'He had the art, in an eminent degree, of inciting the emulation and gaining the affections of his troops'.

By the use of theatrical and emotional language in his Bulletins and Orders of the Day Napoleon formed a special bond between himself and the army. He played on the ideas of military glory, of patriotism and of comradeship, while giving at the same time the impression that he had a deep paternal concern for his men. To this they responded with real devotion. 'The Emperor', he wrote for example in a Bulletin in 1805, 'is among you. He sets the example; he is on horseback day and night; he is amongst his troops, wherever his presence is necessary . . .'. Later in the same campaign he set out to rally the men by allying himself with them: 'Whatever the obstacles we meet we shall overcome them, and we shall not rest until we have planted our banners on the territory of the enemy'. The same campaign finally over, there was a judicious use of praise and promises. 'Soldiers! I am very pleased with you. Today at Austerlitz you have proved that you have the courage which I knew you had . . . I shall lead you back to France and there I shall do all I can to take care of your interests'. Sometimes he played on their greed with promises of material reward in the form of loot. As he said, 'the most important quality in a general is to know the character of his soldiers and to gain their confidence. The military are a Freemasonry, and I am their Grand Master'.

So great was Napoleon's charisma, even in the dark days of 1812, that a sergeant in the Imperial Guard, describing the chaos, suffering and heartbreak of the retreat from Moscow by the tattered, frostbitten remnants of the *Grande Armée*, could afterwards write of himself and those with him:

1 They walked – on frozen feet, leaning on sticks – silently, without complaining, men of all the nations making up our army, covered with cloaks and coats all torn and burnt, wrapped in bits of cloth, in sheepskins, in anything to keep out the cold, holding them-
5 selves as ready as they could for any possible struggle with the enemy . . . The Emperor in our midst – on foot, his baton in his hand . . . he so great, who had made us all so proud of him, inspired us by his glance in this hour of misfortune with confidence and courage, and would find resources to save us yet.
10 There he was – always the great genius; however miserable we might be, with him we were always sure of victory in the end.

Great as his powers of leadership were, they alone could not have won his battles. There are other factors to be considered.

## ii) Other Considerations

### The Changing Nature of War
The majority of eighteenth-century wars were fought with more or less evenly matched, mainly mercenary armies, very similar to each other in training, equipment, composition and strength. Each was quite small, containing sometimes as few as 30,000 men, and the wars were normally undertaken with limited objectives such as the acquisition of a small province, more often than not to be eventually returned after use as a bargaining counter in maintaining the balance of power in the game of international diplomacy.

The great military theorist of the early nineteenth century the Prussian, Clausewitz, had fought in the Revolutionary and Napoleonic wars. In his classic book *On War* published in 1832 he put forward his view that 1793 marked a turning point in the organisation of armies and in the conduct of war. He considered that both were changed for ever by the creation in that year of the French 'nation in arms' (the *levée en masse*) which transformed limited war into total war:

'Perfected by Napoleon military power based on the strength of the whole nation marched over Europe, smashing everything in pieces so surely and certainly, that where it only encountered the old-fashioned armies, the result was not doubtful for a moment'.

The cry of *la patrie en danger* had led in 1792 to the formation of a French national army consisting initially of 'patriotic volunteers'. Universal conscription had long been advocated by such different men as Guibert (the influential and aristocratic pre-Revolutionary military reformer) and Rousseau (the equally influential eighteenth-century philosopher). Both thought it the best way to raise a citizen army which would have wide support, and in 1793 conscription was actually introduced. A year later there were a million men under arms. (France had the advantage of having at that time the largest population in Europe, about 28 million, from which to draw recruits). Although in practice the large majority of conscripts were from poor peasant families, in theory at least universal conscription brought together men from all classes of society in defence of *la patrie*.

Eighteenth-century generals tried to avoid battle, if at all possible, concentrating instead on sieges, or on manoeuvring in order to evade the enemy or to gain a tactical advantage – what Clausewitz called 'diplomacy intensified, a somewhat more vigorous way of negotiating'. Violence was controlled by calm calculation of the risks involved and careful observance of the conventions of war. The enthusiasm and fervour, the *élan* and dash of the Revolutionary armies was something alien to established military practice. The men fighting in the new French armies were not there as mercenaries, nor as men impressed against their will, but as citizens honourably defending *their* Revolution against its threatened destruction by outside forces. Instead of avoiding battle they actively sought it. Often ill-disciplined and ill-equipped, they relied on shock tactics and the momentum of the bayonet charge to bring them success, especially in their early encounters.

The year 1793 was a watershed in other ways than the introduction of conscription – it marked the first *amalgame*, the merging of remnants of the old army with the new. The introduction of veteran soldiers into the new army did much to bring order into its early chaotic organisation without destroying its verve, and formed it into a fighting force which Napoleon used as the basis of his *Grande Armée*.

*The Development of the Grande Armée*

In the period of comparative peace between 1800 and 1804 Napoleon reorganised the French army which under the Directory had been split into a number of separate armies. Each of these had been under the command of a more or less independent general, an arrangement which made concerted action almost impossible. (Napoleon knew this from his own experience – as commander of the Army of Italy and then the Army of Egypt he had frequently made his own decisions and had acted without reference to anyone). His new arrangements were based on the ideas of Guibert, whose thinking was probably the single most important influence on Napoleon's military development. The whole army was divided into corps of about 25–30,000 men; some of the cavalry was kept separate, as were the reserve artillery and several élite groups, the most important of which was the Imperial Guard. The entire army was under the direct and sole control of Napoleon himself, as the commanding general.

The organisational aim was to allow unity of command – Napoleon's – while providing flexibility in action. Each corps was given a particular role on a campaign march, but this role could if necessary be quickly changed; regiments could be transferred from one corps to another if required, and infantry or cavalry detachments could be sent out as skirmishers or moved round as protective screens to shield the movements of the rest of the troops, and leave the enemy confused and uncertain as to what was happening. In battle as well as on the march, flexibility was the key. Once the engagement was joined, the idea was to manoeuvre as would best lure the enemy into taking up an unfavourable position, and then tempt him into committing his whole force, including his reserve, into an all-out attack. Napoleon would at this point order his own reserves to launch a surprise enveloping attack on the enemy's rear and/or flank. In the decisive French charges and relentless pursuit which followed, heavy casualties would be inflicted on the fleeing enemy. These casualties sometimes, as at Marengo, Ulm, Austerlitz and Jena, numbered three times as many as those suffered by the French. This strategy was not new. It had been proposed many years earlier by Guibert, but this does not belittle the brilliance of Napoleon's early victories. To win them he took what had been only a military theory and put it into practice. As Napoleon himself said, 'everything is in the execution'.

*The Development of Winning Tactics*

For some time before the Revolution military strategists had argued about the best way to deploy the principal part of the army, the infantry, on the march or in battle. Should they be in line or column? The column, a long file of soldiers moving slowly along a single road, was the traditional marching formation, but was extremely vulnerable to enemy attack and almost powerless to take offensive action in

emergency. The line abreast was the equally traditional battle formation, three more or less stationary ranks of musketeers firing continuously to order. Well trained, disciplined troops could be very
effective in this formation against infantry or cavalry, but were always
vulnerable to concentrated artillery fire.

In 1791 a compromise was reached between the 'column or line'
schools of thought, and embodied in a new drill manual. This allowed
the commander to choose whatever combination of line and column
seemed best to him at the time, in what came to be called 'mixed order'.
It was a development of this 'mixed order', which Napoleon most
frequently employed in battle – the infantry in a concentrated but
mobile formation made up of both line and column, moving around the
battlefield as required, firing at will, and following up, in Revolutionary
tradition, with a massed bayonet charge when needed, and supported
by the cavalry.

On the march he dispersed his forces into self-contained groups
advancing simultaneously at a distance of perhaps as much as a mile
from each other along several roads, in effect forming a series of
columns in line abreast. This allowed for mutual support and reinforce-
ment in case of attack and at the same time simplified the requisitioning
of supplies from the countryside through which the army was passing.
Following Guibert's precepts once again, Napoleon ensured that the
army should travel light and therefore speedily, covering an average of
12 to 15 miles a day and living off the land instead of relying on slow
supply wagons or on depots requiring careful advance preparation. The
army on the march was, thus, well spread out and extremely mobile,
easily able to move into a loose net-like formation to trap enemy forces
manoeuvring in a traditional compact group. They could then be
rounded up, and forced to fight at a disadavantage. Campaigning for
Napoleon was, until 1807, a successful blend of mobility, speed and
surprise, which brought rich rewards; not until the enemy learnt how to
counter his strategies did the situation change (see page 48).

Like all Revolutionary generals Napoleon was committed to the idea
of the offensive and to the importance of forcing the enemy to give
battle, but only when that enemy had been out-manoeuvred. While he
was able to maintain the surprise element Napoleon won every
encounter. At Ulm in 1805 the Austrians, remaining stationary, were
surrounded. At the twin-battles of Jena-Auerstädt in 1806 the Prussians, on the move, were surrounded and, worse still, found themselves
facing the wrong way as the French attacked and the battle began. It
was a text-book example of the inability of an old-fashioned army to
meet Napoleon on equal terms. The Prussians still operating in
accordance with the teachings of Frederick the Great (most of their
generals had learnt their craft in his campaigns) were organised in slow
and unwieldy line-formation. Restricted in their movement they were
annihilated, losing 45,000 men and all their artillery.

While Napoleon's army remained a national one – the French nation in arms-fighting offensive wars and pursuing a policy of mobility and surprise against the old-fashioned, semi-static armies of the *Ancien Régime*, Clausewitz was right – Napoleon could not lose. In fact, so successful was he in his early campaigns that by his victories he changed the pattern of war. Instead of taking land in the eighteenth-century manner from states in decline (as Poland had been partitioned by her neighbours shortly before the Revolution) he took – and kept – territory belonging to the strong. His victories were so total that diplomats were rendered superfluous to the peace negotiations – he could, and did, dictate his own terms on the vanquished. From 1805 onwards he developed the use of war as *une bonne affaire* (a good thing) financially. Peace treaties imposed on defeated countries not only provided for the free quartering of Napoleon's troops on their territory, but included the payment of massive indemnities – Prussia was forced to find 311 million francs after her defeat at Jena in 1806. War had become satisfactorily self-financing. It would continue to be so for Napoleon, as long as he went on winning.

*Weapons and Training in the Grande Armée*
Armies and their deployment might have changed, but the soldiers' weapons did not begin to do so until the middle of the nineteenth century, when industrial technology caught up with military theory. All Napoleon's campaigns were conducted using the weapons of the *Ancien Régime*. The musket was still the standard infantry weapon – a smooth-bored, muzzle-loading flintlock firing lead bullets, and fitted with a bayonet. Its fire power was limited, its rate of fire slow and its accuracy poor except at close range. The artillery was equally inaccurate and slow, with a range of about half a mile. It took a skilled gun crew to be able to fire a round a minute, even with the new, lighter cannon introduced into France in the 1770s. The use of horse artillery giving greater mobility to the guns, and the new practice of concentrating artillery fire in a barrage to open up gaps in the enemy's front line for infantry or cavalry to attack, were tactics of which Napoleon made good use, especially after 1806 as armies grew larger. They were not, however, his innovations – he had learnt them during his training as a young artillery cadet. In fact he was surprisingly conservative in his military thinking and generally unreceptive to fresh ideas of any kind. He ignored new inventions brought to his attention, such as 'a water waggon driven by fire' (submarine), 'rockets' (incendiaries), the telegraph (a mechanical semaphore system), and the percussion charge (a replacement for the flint-lock). He seems to have known about but to have ignored also the cheap Prussian innovation of a sharp knife attached to a musket which could be used by the infantry to open the cartridges without having to waste time biting them, and so be able to fire more rapidly. He disbanded as unnecessary the small corps of

(ground-anchored) observation balloons used for reconnaisance; but reintroduced for wear by the heavy cavalry the helmet and breastplate, already obsolete in the time of Louis XIV.

Training, to the modern way of thinking, was of the slightest for the new recruit, and continued to follow the programme, intended to combine enthusiasm with discipline, laid down for the Revolutionary armies in the early 1790s. A week in the home base, a hardening-off march of 50 or 60 days to the front, collecting kit, practising drill and gaining experience by example along the way. Most practical training was still provided, especially in a battle situation, by veteran soldiers in the tradition of the *amalgame* (see page 38) of 1793. In 1805, for instance, half the total strength of the army had fought under Napoleon at Marengo (1800), and a quarter had served in the Revolutionary wars; most of the officers and non-commisioned officers were experienced campaigners, although a high proportion of the rank and file were raw conscripts. The army consisted, therefore, of a mixture of old and young, experience and inexperience, combined under one command.

The size of Napoleon's *Grande Armée* (a name which he coined while with the army at Boulogne in 1805) has been disputed at length by military historians. For the years before 1805 estimates vary from about 300,000 upwards. It is now thought, based on the known average figure of 73,000 men enrolled each year in France, that from 1805–6 Napoleon's standing army numbered between 500,000 and 600,000. In addition he had other troops to call on, the auxiliary levies provided by the satellite states, which by 1807 represented about a third of the total strength of his armed forces.

*Napoleon's Strategic Planning*

It used to be stated in campaign histories that Napoleon planned his campaigns and battles well ahead and in meticulous detail, and that his victories came from following his plans minutely; but military historians are now much less certain that this was so. There is some evidence on this point from Napoleon himself, when, in 1804 and in rather boastful vein, he declared:

1 Military science consists in calculating all the chances accurately in the first place and then giving accident, almost mathematically, its place in one's calculations. It is upon this point that one must not deceive oneself and that a fraction more or less may change
5 everything. Now the apportioning of accident and science cannot get into any head, except that of a genius . . . Accident, luck, chance, whatever you choose to call it – a mystery to ordinary minds – becomes a reality to superior minds.

A couple of years later he wrote to his brother Joseph that 'in war nothing is achieved except by calculation. Everything that is not soundly planned in its detail yields no result'.

Recent reassessments of Napoleon's military career suggest that while he had always formulated a general plan, whether for a whole campaign or a particular battle – 'my great talent, the one that distinguishes me the most, is to see the *whole* picture distinctly' – he was basically an opportunist, prepared to adjust his plans according to changing circumstances and to take advantage of enemy errors or weakness. He could improvise brilliantly in the heat of battle and frequently did so, abandoning his original plan without hesitation. He was, however, always unwilling to take others into his confidence. This habit of keeping his ideas to himself resulted in a weakness of the command structure, which was to have serious results in later years.

In the same way, the old idea that Napoleon was forever moving his troops from one place to another, making in the process lightning marches across Europe, has been discredited. Such marches, like the famous one from the Channel coast to the Danube in 1805, were the exception. When he needed to Napoleon could organise the rapid movement of large numbers of men over wide areas to converge on his chosen target, but normally his marches were shorter, slower and less dramatic.

Whether he had 'a grand strategy' in the sense of a wide, overall design for the war as a whole is difficult to say. The only consistent theme running through the years from 1800–15 is enmity for Britain. Until 1805, it is suggested, his 'grand strategy' may have involved a naval confrontation with Britain, but if so it, as well as the proposed invasion plans, had to be abandoned as the result of the heavy French losses at Trafalgar. Napoleon's relations with his navy were never happy or successful, he had no admiral to compare with Nelson, and no understanding of ships nor liking for the sea. He therefore concentrated from 1805 onwards on dealing with his enemies on land, while keeping up an attack on Britain by means of the Continental Blockade (see page 113).

*iii) Napoleon's Generalship – an Assessment*
Many historians are no longer ready to accept unquestioningly that Napoleon was a great general. They point out that he was in no way an innovator. He made no significant contribution to tactics, introduced no new weapons and was not open to new ideas. His contributions to strategy were not original. The armies he commanded were taken over from the Revolution, the *levée en masse* was established before he came to power. He introduced no new training methods. He underestimated supply problems, and made other errors of judgement, often because of his amazing, but unacknowledged, ignorance of climatic and geographical conditions. This led to avoidable losses in Egypt and in San Dominigue from heat and fever, from cold, snow, and mud on other

occasions, the crossing of the Oder in 1806 for instance. Sometimes out of sheer obstinacy, as at Boulogne in 1805, he refused advice from those who knew better than to underestimate as he did the dangers to his ships from tide and weather. His lack of interest in the provision of maps covering the terrain over which he was to march, his often inadequate reconnaissance, and his failure to appreciate the difference between foraging in the prosperous and well-populated west of Europe and in the bare lands further east caused his men unnecessary hardship, as did his reduction of the army medical services to save money. He may have declared that the men's health was of paramount importance to him, but the sick and wounded on campaign were left to die.

Despite these well founded criticsms, there are historians who still believe that Napoleon was nevertheless a great general. They quote Wellington who thought that he was 'a great *homme de guerre* , possibly the greatest who ever appeared at the head of a French army'. They point out the extent of Napoleon's conquests achieved in so few years, and write that Napoleon's 'military genius has never been surpassed', that he was 'one of the world's four greatest commanders', and that 'his campaigns have been made a text-book of military science'.

This reputation rests largely on the successes of his early campaigns in Italy and Egypt, and on the those of 1805–6, when he was still young and energetic, full of enthusiasm and, it seemed, invincible. His methods, if not exactly new in theory, were new in practice and he used them well. They were a break with eighteenth-century tradition, and confusing to the opposition. Given his hold over his men and the incapacity of his enemies to match him and his army, his victories multiplied rapidly. If his career had finished in, say, 1807, it would have been one of undisputed military glory, justifying his admirers' plaudits. But it did not finish then, and the failures and defeats of the later years, the blunders and ill-judged decisions of the later campaigns, in Spain, in Russia, even at Waterloo, must be taken into account in painting the overall picture of Napoleon as a military leader.

## b) Napoleon's Strength – the Civil Aspect

In considering Napoleon's strength the civil aspect should not be forgotten. When he became First Consul Napoleon took over the existing ministry of war, expanded it and made it more efficient. It was reorganised into two separate ministries, one dealing with the army itself (conscription, promotions, troop movements and the like) and one concerned with administration (provisions, supplies and military transport). The real power, though, lay with the war section of the Council of State, all decisions of which were made by Napoleon himself.

In the absolutist state which he created, Napoleon's resources for war were unrivalled in Europe. Money, men and materials were his to demand, the plans his to make. By breaking with Revolutionary principles and uniting in himself the offices of head of state and active commander-in-chief of the army there was no conflict of civil and military interests, for he alone made the decisions. It was a situation not enjoyed by any enemy general.

## c) The Enemies' Weakness – Allied Disunity

Britain, Russia, Austria and later Prussia formed a series of anti-French alliances with each other, but these were continually undermined by their mutual suspicions and jealousy. Only Britain remained opposed to France for the whole period. The other three powers were tempted away from time to time by Napoleon's offers of territory, for as well as making use of the opportunity to profit from quarrels among the allies, Napoleon's foreign policy was based on 'divide and rule'. His normal strategy was to keep at least one of these major powers as an ally while he dealt with the others.

### i) The Second Coalition 1799

In the spring of 1799 the Second Coalition of Britain, Russia, Austria and the Ottoman Empire was at war with France. Theoretically a strong combination, it was in fact nothing of the sort. It was not in fact an overall coalition, but a series of separate alliances, and even these links were not complete for there was no alliance between Britain and Austria. Even more important there was no agreement on a unified military strategy, nor was there a commitment by the allies not to make a separate peace with France if it suited their interests to do so. Although Austrian and Russian forces pushed the French out of Italy in the summer of 1799, (this was part of the news which brought Napoleon hurrying back from Egypt and precipitated the *coup d'état* of Brumaire), an Anglo-Russian landing in Holland was unsuccessful and led to recriminations between the British and Russian commanders over whose fault it was that they had been defeated.

Relations between the two countries worsened over the question of control over French-held Malta, at that time being blockaded by Britain but promised by her to Russia in due course. At the same time a rift developed between Austria and the other two powers over Austrian suspicions of British intentions in Belgium and Russian ambitions in Italy. These differences exposed the much deeper divisions among the allies on the whole nature of the war against France. Russia was unsympathetic to the British view that the fight was one to destroy the Revolution totally, while Austria favoured the eighteenth-century view of the conflict as a limited one which would end in an exchange of territory – perhaps Belgium for Sardinia. The defeat of the Russian army by the French near Zurich in September 1799 led to the break-up of the Coalition, from which the Tsar withdrew in November of that year.

Over the winter of 1799–1800 Napoleon, now First Consul, tried with some success to win Tsar Paul over to his side, while also attempting to make peace with Austria and Britain. As the two allies could not agree between themselves what would be an equitable settlement, it proved impossible to reach an agreement. As a result, Napoleon decided that if France was to have peace he would have to impose it, but to do this he would have to defeat one of the allies first. Therefore he embarked on a second Italian campaign aimed against Austria, and forced her to accept the humiliating loss of all her Italian possessions, except Venice, at the Peace of Lunéville (February 1801). Meanwhile, Tsar Paul, irritated by Britain's refusal to give up Malta and by her high-handed behaviour over the interpretation of some aspects of maritime law, had formed a League of Armed Neutrality (Russia, Sweden, Denmark and Prussia) to keep Britain out of the Baltic. Although the assassination of the Tsar in March 1801 and Nelson's bombardment of Copenhagen the following month brought the League to a speedy end, the new Tsar, Alexander I, despite his anti-French sympathies, showed no signs of wishing to form an Anglo-Russian alliance. Isolated and tired of war, Britain had little choice but to accept the Peace of Amiens in March 1802.

## ii) The Third Coalition 1805
In May 1803, after six months of deteriorating international relations, Britain declared war on France. However, there was little that Britain, with a strong navy but a very small army, could do on her own. In 1804 William Pitt, who had become Prime Minister since the resumption of hostilities, began the search for allies to join a Third Coalition. He announced his willingness to pay subsidies on an unprecedented scale to any ally willing to provide the troops needed to fight Napoleon on the continent, but neither Russia, Austria nor Prussia came forward. Austria and Russia were both anxious to see Napoleon defeated, but were not prepared to work together, for each still blamed the other for deserting the Second Coalition in 1799. In addition, Russia was not prepared to co-operate with Britain because the question of Malta was still unresolved.

By the middle of 1805 evidence of Napoleon's enormous ambitions, his assumption of the title of Emperor and of King of Italy combined to persuade Russia and Austria to join Britain in the Third Coalition. The coalition was fragile from the beginning because once again there was no overall treaty uniting the three powers, and because each of the members again had different wishes for the outcome of the war. This time the Tsar dreamed of a crusade for peace in Europe and an extension of Russian influence in south-east Europe, Austria aimed to recover her position in Italy and Germany, while Britain still wanted the comprehensive defeat of France. Attempts to persuade Prussia to join the Coalition had failed – Napoleon's tempting offer of Hanover (French since 1803) in return for neutrality had been too attractive. This use of Hanover had been a shrewd move by Napoleon, as the territory had previously belonged to George III and its 'passing on' was bound to cause friction between Britain and Prussia.

Austria did not remain a member of the coalition for long. In October her army was defeated at Ulm and she made a separate peace with France. Prussia, resentful of pressure from Napoleon to supply him with troops and to join the Continental Blockade against Britain, eventually declared war on France in August 1806. However, her adherence to the coalition was as shortlived as Austria's had been. Her army was totally defeated in October at the twin battles of Jena-Auerstädt. The most powerful army of the *Ancien Régime* had been destroyed by Napoleon's new style warfare.

Britain's other ally, Russia, had become involved in a distracting war with the Ottoman Empire by the end of 1806. Taking advantage of this, Napoleon launched an attack through Poland, and in the spring of 1807 won a decisive victory over the Russians at Friedland. Afterwards he was able to exploit the Tsar's resentment over the inactivity of Britain and Austria and the poor military showing by Prussia during 1806. At their private meetings at Tilsit in June 1807 Napoleon entirely capti-vated Alexander, who formally allied himself with France. Prussia and Austria were left to the mercy of Napoleon. Both emerged greatly weakened from the peace settlement, losing influence and territory and being burdened with the payment of heavy war indemnities to France. The Third Coalition was dead. Only Britain, which since 1805 had played no part in Europe other than that of pay-master, still remained at war with France. Once again Napoleon had succeeded admirably in playing on divisions between the allies, and then in picking them off one by one.

## 2  Decline and Fall 1808–15

Although the frontiers of 1807 are not those of the Empire at its greatest extent, that year does mark an important turning point in Napoleon's affairs. He can be said at that time to have been at the peak of success, with his three mainland enemies brought to heel, and with the expectation that Britain would soon succumb to the Continental Blockade. In November 1807 Russia declared war on her former ally, Britain. Any further anti-French coalition was obviously impossible for the time being. Napoleon would never again be so well placed to dominate Europe. There were still victories to come and conquests to be made, but only at an increased cost in men and materials and with greater difficulty; and there were to be disasters and defeats. The general trend from 1808 onwards was no longer upward. Decline did not, however, set in immediately.

## a) The Military Situation

There were changes in the armies and methods of warfare of both Napoleon and his enemies after 1807. In that year the *Grande Armée* was still strong enough to defeat all who stood in its way, Austrians, Prussians, or Russians. It had, however, lost many of its experienced and disciplined troops and, although new recruits were available to fill the gaps, they went into battle untrained and often unreliable. As a result, Napoleon's earlier tactics of attack by columns of infantry were no longer so successful and he began to rely much more on sustained artillery barrages. As his armies became larger – over 600,000 crossed the Niemen into Russia with him in 1812 – they were more difficult to manoeuvre and to provision on the march. His later campaigns had, therefore, to depend much less on the surprise elements of speed and mobility than before, and his battles to rely much more on the sheer brute force of artillery duels or the weight of numbers storming the enemy lines in a massed charge of cavalry or infantry. His later victories were much costlier in men than the earlier ones. For example, 30,000 were lost at Wagram in 1809 compared with the 8,000 lost at Austerlitz in 1805. French losses overall in the Austrian campaign of 1809 were almost equal to those of the enemy.

While the rest of Europe continued to employ old-fashioned methods Napoleon's new style armies had been invincible. This situation did not last. His enemies learnt to play Napoleon at his own game. They copied his tactics, became more flexible, and developed their artillery to match his. They increased the size of their armies to equal or exceed his. The French army had been created as a national army, but by 1807 its character had changed. It had become increasingly cosmopolitan Two-thirds of the men were either non-French troops from the annexed territories or foreign auxiliaries from the satellite states of the Grand Empire. Ironically it was just at this time that Prussia and Austria, after their disastrous defeats, began replacing their old foreign mercenary armies with new national ones, designed to have a 'new structure, armament and equipment in accordance with the new methods of warfare'. By adopting new methods and by learning how to pin Napoleon down to a more defensive style of warfare, by denying him the opportunity to force an early and, he hoped, decisive battle, and in the end by co-operating among themselves long enough to be able to field a combined force of superior manpower, the allies at last learnt how to defeat Napoleon.

To some extent Napoleon played into their hands by the 'mistakes' of the Spanish and Russian ventures, brought about by his determination to force both countries to implement the Continental Blockade against

Britain (see page 25). In both cases he grossly underestimated the sheer size of the country he was hoping to conquer, and was ill-informed about both the terrain or the climate he would encounter. Accustomed to allowing his armies to 'live off the land' in countries they were campaigning in, he wrongly expected they could also do so in Spain and Russia. In Spain guerrilla fighters, and in Russia scorched earth policies, produced unexpected difficulties for the French troops. The 'Spanish ulcer' eventually cost Napoleon about 300,000 men and 3000 million francs in gold, and brought the first serious defeats for his armies. In Russia matters were even worse: nearly 500,000 men dead, missing or taken prisoner, and 200,000 trained horses and 1000 guns lost – all in the course of a campaign lasting only six months. This enormous expenditure of experienced officers and men weakened the French army, especially the cavalry, for future campaigns, leaving it over-dependent on new levies of raw recruits. Even more important was that the disasters of 1812 and the defeats in the Peninsular War shattered Napoleon's reputation for military invincibility.

It had always been a weakness in his command structure that he did not take his senior officers into his confidence when on campaign, nor allow them any independence of action. He retained all power and all decision-making in his own hands. It was an entirely personal leadership. In the early campaigns when his army was still quite small this did not matter a great deal, but as armies became larger – already in 1806 Napoleon was at the head of an army at Jena of about 165,000 men – personal control over the entire field of operations became more difficult to achieve. Even then Napoleon did not establish a permanent staff to share the command. He continued to tell his marshals what to do, and they continued to do it. As one of them remarked, 'the Emperor needs neither advice nor plans of campaign . . . our duty is just to obey'. As a result when, as in Spain for instance, they were unavoidably left in charge in Napoleon's absence from the country, his senior staff proved quite unable to cope on their own.

Caulincourt, one of Napoleon's trusted generals, who travelled everywhere with him on campaign, riding alongside his carriage as a privileged member of his entourage, and who knew as much as anybody was ever permitted to know about the Emperor, wrote illuminatingly of his strengths and weaknesses in the field:

1 On campaign he was awakened for everything. Even the Chief of
    Staff who received and despatched and knew the Emperor's
    plans, decided nothing . . . The Emperor occupied himself with
    the most minute details. He wanted everything to bear the
5   imprint of his genius. He would send for me to receive his orders
    for headquarters, for the orderly officers, for his staff officers, for
    the letters, for the couriers, the postal service . . . The comman-
    ding officers of the guard; the controller of the army commisariat;

the surgeon-general were all summoned to him at least once a day.
10 Nothing escaped his care . . . no detail seemed too humble to
escape his attention. He had an astonishing memory for localities
. . . The distinctive numbers of his regiments, his army service
companies, his baggage battalions were all classified in his brain
most marvellously. He knew where each one was, when it started
15 and when it should arrive at its destination. Never did a man
combine such a memory with a more creative genius.

   But his creative genius had no knowledge of conserving its
forces. Always improvising, in a few days he would consume,
exhaust and disorganise, by his marches, the whole of what his
20 genius had created. If a thirty-days' campaign did not produce the
results of a year's fighting, the greater part of his calculations were
upset by the losses he suffered, for everything was done so rapidly
and unexpectedly, the chiefs under him had so little experience,
showed so little care and were, in addition, so spoiled by former
25 successes, that everything was disorganised, wasted and thrown
away . . . The prompt results of the Italian and Austrian campaigns and the resources those countries offered to the invader
spoiled everyone, down to the least important commanders, for
more rigorous warfare. This habit of victory cost us dear when we
30 got to Russia and even dearer when we were in retreat; the
glorious habit of marching ever forward made us veritable
schoolboys when it came to retreating.

   In a similar vein, Metternich, the Austrian Chancellor, wrote of what
he saw as the major reason for Napoleon's initial success and eventual
failure:

1 Napoleon did not fail to reckon largely on the weakness and
   errors of his adversaries. It must be confessed that a long
   experience only too well justified him in following this principle.
   But it is also certain that he abused it, and that the habit of
5 despising the means and capabilities of his adversaries was one of
   the principle causes of his downfall. The Alliance of 1813
   destroyed him, because he was never able to persuade himself
   that the members of a coalition could remain united and persevere
   in a given course of action.

By 1814 Napoleon's early self-confidence and determination had
degenerated into supreme egoism, obstinacy and an unwillingness to
face facts – a fatal combination for a commander about to meet for the
first time a united enemy able to deploy a numerically superior
combined force.

## b) The Allies United

### i) *The Fourth Coalition 1813–15*

The Russian debacle encouraged a general diplomatic reshuffle, which began in February 1813 with the signing of an anti-French alliance by Russia and Prussia. Tsar Alexander now saw himself as the saviour of Europe. He believed he had a Christian mission to complete the defeat of Napoleon and to free Europe from tyranny. Under his leadership the Fourth Coalition, initially composed of Russia, Prussia and Britain, was formed in 1813. It was still not a full, united alliance, being based only on separate bilateral treaties between Britain and Russia and Britain and Prussia. In the early summer of 1813 a Russo-Prussian campaign in central Europe met with some success and in June Napoleon – with a much weakened army after his losses in Russia, and forced to fight on two fronts by the continued conflict in Spain – accepted Austrian proposals for an armistice and a peace conference. Austria's attitude towards the Fourth Coalition had so far been one of hesitant suspicion. The Chancellor, Metternich, distrusted Russo-Prussian ambitions in Germany, and Napoleon's marriage to Marie-Louise had left Austria in an awkward position as a nominal ally of France, but in August 1813 Austria, tired of Napoleon's unwillingness to negotiate a peace settlement, declared war on France. It was the first occasion on which *all* the other great powers, Britain, Russia, Prussia and Austria, were at war with Napoleon at the same time; but there was still no single alliance binding them together.

The end of the armistice led to renewed fighting, and in October the numerical superiority of the combined armies of Austria, Prussia and Russia enabled them to win a decisive but expensive victory at Leipzig in the three-day 'Battle of the Nations'. With the loss of the battle, Napoleon also lost control over Germany and was forced to retreat to the Rhine and the defence of the 'natural frontiers' of France. Napoleon's only hope was that Austria, Prussia and Russia would quarrel over the future of Germany and Poland and that the coalition would collapse as a result. This was Britain's fear, but it was averted when intense diplomatic pressure by the British government led to the imposition of the Treaty of Chaumont on the coalition in March 1814. This treaty, which converted the coalition into a Quadruple Alliance, committed each of the four powers not to conclude a separate peace, but to fight on until Napoleon was defeated. They would then remain in alliance for 20 years while political and territorial plans, outlined in the treaty, were put into effect in a post-Napoleonic Europe. At long last the allies had come together in a properly united alliance of powers legally bound to each other in a common purpose.

### ii) *Final Defeat and the End of Napoleonic Europe*

The Grand Empire collapsed very quickly after the Battle of the

Nations in 1813. It had always depended on military supremacy. That lost, the satellite states began to desert Napoleon. Several minor states actually went over to the allies in return for promises to respect their sovereignty.

At the end of March 1814 an allied advance captured Paris, and in April Napoleon abdicated unconditionally as Emperor of the French. The first Treaty of Paris (May 1814) began the long process of reaching a peace settlement by reducing France to her 1792 borders. Almost immediately after the treaty was signed the allies fell out with one another. Matters became so acrimonious that Britain and Austria, encouraged by the restored Bourbon government of France, made a secret alliance against Prussia and Russia. The Coalition was only saved by the sudden return of Napoleon from Elba in March 1815 and the need to restore the war-time co-operation. This was successfully achieved, enabling Britain and Prussia to join forces at the battle of Waterloo. After Napoleon's final abdication and exile in June, the second Treaty of Paris (November 1815) reduced the frontiers of France still further to those of 1790.

There remained the problem of the territories of the French Empire and of the satellite states. Each of the allies had different views on what should be done and great power unity was constantly threatened by suspicion and disagreement. However, it was accepted by all the allies that France needed to be contained within her revised frontiers and that this could be best done by surrounding her with a ring of buffer states – not the weak and feeble neighbours who had collapsed in 1792–3, but strong, potentially hostile states who would prevent any future French aggression. To the south, Austrian influence was restored in northern Italy in Lombardy and Venice, and a newly strengthened kingdom of Sardinia-Piedmont (including Nice, Genoa and Savoy) guarded the Italian frontier with France; to the north, Belgium was united with an independent Holland behind a fortified frontier with France; while to the east, Switzerland's guaranteed independence barred the way, as did the Rhinelands, now a part of Prussia. In this way the frontiers which France had threatened most often during the seventeenth and eighteenth centuries were blocked off.

As far as the satellite states were concerned it was a generally, though not completely, conservative settlement. In Italy Naples was returned to Bourbon rule and the other states were restored to their pre-1796 boundaries and mostly to their former ruling families. The Papal States were returned to the Pope. In Germany Napoleon's suppression of a large number of minor German states was confirmed and 41 (later reduced to 38) sovereign states were brought together in a new German Confederation, whose borders were not dissimilar to those of the old Holy Roman Empire. Russia acquired most of Poland and Spain was returned to Bourbon rule.

The map of Europe again looked much the same as it had done in the eighteenth century. Geographically, Napoleonic Europe had disappeared. Whether anything else of it remained after 1815 will be discussed in the next chapter.

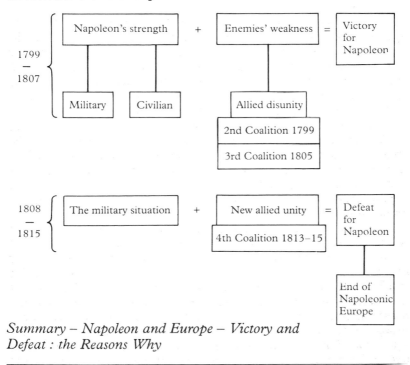

*Summary – Napoleon and Europe – Victory and Defeat : the Reasons Why*

---

### Making notes on 'Napoleon and Europe – Victory and Defeat: The Reasons Why'

This chapter looks at Napoleon's strengths and weaknesses as a military commander, and the reasons for his early victories and later defeats. While it is very unusual for an examination question to be set on a specific campaign, Napoleon's military achievements must form part of any answer which deals with the rise and fall of the Empire. In the same way, while detailed knowledge of successive allied coalitions is not called for, it is important to understand the part played in Napoleon's success by allied disunity prior to the Fourth Coalition – and why the situation changed after it was formed.

This chapter is important, for many general questions on Napoleon's career (examples of which are to be found at the end of chapter 8) need solid information on his military prowess as well as his domestic achievements. Using the following plan for making your notes should prove helpful in clarifying your ideas:

1 Victory 1800–7
  i) Napoleon's Strength
    a) Military Aspect
      (What were his strategies? Was he an innovator? Why did he win, so easily, so many battles? What was the character of his army? How good a military leader was he?)
    b) Civil Aspect
      (What gave him the edge over other military leaders?)
  ii) The Enemies' Weakness
    (Why was the enemy so disunited? What made the Second and Third Coalitions so weak?)

2 Defeat 1808–15
  i) Changes in the Military Situation
    (What were these changes? Were they due to Napoleon? or to others?)
  ii) The Enemy United
    (How and why did this happen? What made the Fourth Coalition different?)
  iii) The Final Defeat
    (What became of the Empire after 1815? What were the frontiers of France?)

---

*Answering essay questions on 'Napoleon and Europe – Victory and Defeat: The Reasons Why'*

Historians are continually reappraising Napoleon's military reputation. Very few would now accept wholeheartedly the idea that 'his military genius was unsurpassed' or that 'he was probably the greatest military leader of all time'. Most are much more restrained. While they admire his early campaigns, they are careful to draw attention to his later mistakes and failures. Therefore, when you are faced with questions such as

1 Does Napoleon deserve his traditional reputation as a great military leader? or
2 Write a critical appraisal of Napoleon as a military commander

try to present a balanced a picture in the main part of your essay. Indicate what historians, past and present, have thought about Napoleon as a military commander but be prepared to state your own opinions on Napoleon's military ability, with supporting evidence, in the course of your conclusion.

The majority of questions on Napoleon's military activities in Europe are relatively straightforward:

3  Why was Napoleon able to conquer so much of Europe so easily?
4  Why was Napoleon not defeated in Europe until 1814?
5  How and why did Napoleon's power in Europe decline?
6  Why were Napoleon's successes against the Third Coalition followed by his defeat by the Fourth Coalition?
7  Why was Napoleon so successful against his enemies between 1799 and 1807?
8  Why did Napoleon finally fail in the conquest of Europe?
9  Why has Borodino been called the turning point in Napoleon's military career?

To answer some of these questions you may find it helpful to refer back to the previous chapter.

The main difficulty with questions such as these is to avoid the pitfall of descriptive narrative, for it is very easy to write long answers of a kind which gain comparatively few marks. Often this is because the actual question asked has not been answered directly. In question 6, for example, the temptation is to write at length about Napoleon's successes against the Third Coalition and his defeat by the Fourth Coalition while paying scant attention to the point at issue – *why* did these things happen. What are the 'temptations' in the other questions in this section?

---

*Source-based questions on 'Napoleon and Europe – Victory and Defeat: the Reasons Why'*

## 1 Napoleon's Military Leadership

Carefully read the series of extracts on pages 36–38, 42–43 and 49–50. Answer the following questions.

a) To what (pages 36–38 and 42–43) did Napoleon and his contemporaries attribute his successful military leadership? (*5 marks*)

b) To what (pages 42–43) did Napoleon on this occasion attribute it? How far are military historians in agreement with this view? (*5 marks*)

c) In the extract on pages 49–50 what did Caulincourt identify as Napoleon's strengths and weaknesses? Explain what he meant by 'the glorious habit of marching ever forward made us veritable schoolboys when it came to retreating'. (*5 marks*)

d) What did Metternich (page 50) see as Napoleon's major weakness? How far does his analysis agree with that of Caulincourt? (*5 marks*)

# CHAPTER 5

# Napoleon and the Empire

## 1 The Development of the Empire

The Empire had its official birth on 18 May 1804, with the proclamation of Napoleon as hereditary Emperor of the French, and received its religious blessing six months later on the occasion of Napoleon's coronation at Notre Dame in the presence of the Pope. Its unofficial life, though, had begun long before 1804, with the Revolutionary quests (see page 20) and those of the Consulate (see page 23). Both of these had pushed the frontiers of 'old France' (the France of 1790) out towards her 'natural frontiers' – and beyond.

The 'Empire' is often referred to as if it were a single entity embracing all French-controlled Europe. It was a more complicated arrangement than that. The French Empire properly speaking was France of the natural frontiers (Rhine, Alps, Pyrenees) plus the annexed territories (*pays réunis* ruled from Paris) of Piedmont, Parma, Tuscany, the Papal States, the Illyrian Provinces and, after 1810, Holland. A semi-circle of nominally independent satellite states, (*pays conquis*) ruled by Frenchmen, usually Bonaparte relatives, formed a buffer zone protecting the borders of the French Empire from attack. These states, combined with the French Empire proper, formed the Grand Empire. In the west, the satellites included at various times Switzerland, the kingdoms of Spain, Naples, and Italy; Napoleon's Germanic Confederation of the Rhine (of which the kingdom of Westphalia formed part) and, until 1810, Holland. In eastern Europe there was the Grand Duchy of Warsaw which had been created out of the conquered Polish lands as a barrier to Russian expansion into central Europe. (See page 57 for a reference list of the Imperial Territories, and the map on page 26). There were also a small group of allied states (*pays alliés*) in the Confederation of the Rhine which were ruled by their native sovereigns but owed allegiance to Napoleon. Included in these states was Saxony, whose king was given oversight of the Grand Duchy of Warsaw by Napoleon. Of the great powers, Austria, Prussia and Russia were each from time to time brought by military or diplomatic pressures into Napoleon's direct sphere of influence and each in turn became his ally, though not always willingly and only for a limited period. Even the outlying Baltic powers came within Napoleon's orbit when he involved them in operating the Continental Blockade – Sweden, much weakened by the loss of Finland to Russia as the result of an attack instigated by France, fared particularly badly and had in 1810 to accept a Napoleonic marshal as heir to the Swedish throne. In Europe only the Ottoman Empire and Britain remained always outside Napoleon's control.

## Territories of the Empire – A Reference List

### Revolutionary Period 1790–9
1790 'Old France', 83 departments, 28 million inhabitants
1791 23 military divisions created
**Territories Annexed:**
1791 Avignon
1792 Savoy
1793 Nice
1795 Belgium and Luxemburg
1798 German left bank of the Rhine
**'Sister Republics' Created:**
1795 Batavian Republic (Holland)
1797 Cisalpine Republic (North Italy) became Republic of Italy
   1801
1797 Ligurian Republic (Genoa)
1798 Helvetic Republic (Switzerland)

### Consulate Period 1799–1804
1800 France (including Belgium), 98 departments, 33 million
   inhabitants
**Territories Annexed:**
1802 Piedmont (conquered 1796–7) now formally annexed
1803 Swiss Confederation reorganised with Napoleon as
   'Mediator'

### The Empire Period 1804–14
1804 108 departments
**Territories Annexed:**
1805 Ligurian Republic
1808 Parma and Kingdom of Etruria (Grand Duchy of Tuscany
   created for Napoleon's sister Elise 1809)
1809 Papal States (the part not already included 1808 in satellite
   Kingdom of Italy). Rome named 'second city of Empire'
   1810
1809 Illyrian Provinces
1810 Kingdom of Holland annexed (Napoleon considered Louis
   to be too lenient with the Dutch to remain king of a satellite
   Holland)
1811 The Hansa towns of Hamburg, Bremen and Lübeck, and
   Duchy of Oldenburg
**Satellite states created:**
1805 Kingdom of Italy created out of Republic of Italy with
   Napoleon as king, but ruled by Eugène de Beauharnais,
   Napoleon's stepson, as viceroy
1806 Venetia incorporated into Kingdom of Italy

1806 Kingdom of Naples created with Napoleon's brother Joseph as king

1806 Kingdom of Holland created out of Batavian Republic with Napoleon's brother Louis as king (until annexed in 1810)

1806 Confederation of the Rhine formed with Napoleon as 'Protector'. Holy Roman Empire abolished. The Confederation initially had 16 member states – later others were incorporated including the kingdoms of Saxony and Westphalia

1807 Kingdom of Westphalia created, partly from Prussian and Hanoverian territory, with Napoleon's brother Jérôme as king

1807 Portugal subjugated; French general appointed governor 1808

1807 Grand Duchy of Warsaw created out of the conquered Polish lands and given to the king of Saxony to administer

1808 Kingdom of Spain created and Napoleon's brother Joseph moved from Naples to be king. Joachim Murat, husband of Napoleon's sister, Caroline, made king of Naples

1808 Papal States (part) incorporated into Kingdom of Italy

1809 Trentino and South Tyrol incorporated into Kingdom of Italy

1810 Remainder of Hanover (occupied by French since 1804) ceded to Kingdom of Westphalia, although the best lands were detached and given to Napoleon's *Domaine extraordinaire*

1810 French influence extended into the Baltic by the appointment of the Napoleonic marshal Bernadotte as Crown Prince of Sweden and heir to the throne, and by Scandinavian involvement in the Continental Blockade

1811 Napoleon's European territories reached their greatest extent:
The French Empire (i.e. France of the natural frontiers plus the annexed territories) contained 130 departments, 44 million inhabitants, 32 military divisions
The Grand Empire (i.e. the French Empire plus the satellite states) contained over 80 million inhabitants

## 2 Napoleon and the Conquered Territories

What was Napoleon's purpose in creating the Empire, what did he expect from it and what did he provide for its people in return?

The states of the Grand Empire fell into one of two categories – lands annexed directly to France, or satellite states under French control but allegedly enjoying a modicum of independence. Treatment varied according to which category a state came into. The extent of Napoleonic influence varied too, depending on the length of time a particular country remained under his authority. Historians are in general agreement that the greatest impact was felt, as might be expected, in those annexed regions which were closest to France itself and which were longest subject to her laws.

## a)  The Annexed Territories

Among the annexed territories Nice, Savoy, Belgium and the German lands west of the Rhine had the longest period of French control. They had been annexed early, all before 1799, and had been quickly incorporated into the French administrative system, being divided into departments for civil affairs and into military divisions for recruiting purposes. By the time of Brumaire, feudalism had been abolished in these territories as it had been in France. Feudal dues were done away with, and property and lands belonging to the nobility or church were confiscated and sold. In 1802 Piedmont, under French occupation since 1796, was formally annexed, as was the Ligurian Republic in 1805. Ruled from Paris, all these states came to be regarded as territorial extensions of the 'old France', and an integral part of the new Napoleonic France. All the national institutions flourished there: the Concordat and the Civil Code, the Imperial University, the judicial process of civil and criminal courts, and rather less welcomely, the taxation system and liability for conscription.

Recent research on conditions in these annexed territories has concentrated not so much on legal, economic and administrative changes brought about there, as on looking at the evidence for an underlying social and economic continuity from pre- to post-Napoleonic times. In Piedmont, for instance, where there had been a considerable degree of defeudalisation before the French conquests of 1796–7, and where freehold property was already a common form of land tenure, it is now thought that the introduction of French law brought little new and simply gave legal sanction to an existing situation. In the economically developed lands on the west bank of the Rhine the bourgeoisie are now known to have been both adaptable to the new, and tenacious of the past. They fell in first with the wishes of their French rulers and after 1815 with those of their new masters, the Prussians, while managing at the same time to defend and maintain their pre-Napoleonic social status along with their old trade privileges, traditional local customs and commercial interests.

Those German and Italian territories which were annexed later (see Reference List page 57) had obviously a much shorter time before 1814 in which to adjust to French law and practice and were neither as profoundly nor as longlastingly affected by the changes introduced by Napoleon. Indeed recent research suggests that in these territories social structure did not change much from that of the old régimes.

## b) The Satellite States

The satellite states, allegedly independent, in fact had little freedom of action. From the beginning their rulers were strictly supervised and tutored by Napoleon in the way they should go:
    Napoleon's stepson, Eugène de Beauharnais was told:

1 By entrusting you with the government of Our Kingdom of Italy
  we have given you proof of the respect which your conduct has
  inspired in Us. But you are still at an age [23] when one does not
  realise the perversity of men's hearts: I cannot therefore recom-
5 mend too strongly prudence and circumspection . . . let no one
  have your complete confidence and never tell anyone what you
  think . . . Dissimulation has to be emphasised . . . If you ever find
  yourself speaking . . . from the heart, say to yourself 'I have made
  a mistake' and don't do it again. The less you talk the better . . .
10 learn to listen and remember that silence is often as effective as a
  display of knowledge: however much people flatter you, they all
  know your limitations . . . So long as a prince holds his tongue,
  his power is incalcuable

When the new Kingdom of Westphalia was established in 1807, Napoleon's brother Jérôme was similarly treated. The letter of instruction put him firmly in his place. It began uncompromisingly:

I enclose the constitution for your kingdom. The constitution
contains the conditions on which I renounce all the rights of
conquest and all the claims I have acquired over your kingdom.
You must observe it faithfully.

Over and over again Napoleon wrote to his brothers setting out his fervent desire for the well-being of the imperial subjects – 'The aim of your administration is the happiness of My Italian peoples . . . count yourself a failure unless the Italians believe you love them'; 'I am concerned for the happiness of your subjects [in Westphalia]'; but this was mere window-dressing. Napoleon was not concerned with fostering the simple happiness of the common people, nor, despite his assertions, with encouraging the spread of liberty and equality by actively ending feudalism throughout the Empire. Evidence is now available that feudalism was abolished more in legal principle than in actuality in the satellite states, and that it survived in many areas in its old form of noble privileges, feudal dues, serfdom and even labour services. This suggests that the traditional text book statements that Napoleon defeudalised his European conquests need to be modified. At best his achievements in this direction seem to have been patchy and largely restricted to the countries annexed early. A recently published analysis of Continental research on the subject indicates that 'part of Napoleon's reforms remained more talked about than done' and that he in effect settled for a pragmatic compromise with the traditional feudal structures of the satellite states. It now seems likely that pre-Napoleonic noble or bourgeois élitist groups continued to survive in sufficient numbers for the social structure to remain largely unchanged in much of Italy, Germany and in Poland. This, it can be argued, was one reason why the Empire collapsed so quickly in 1814, and why the allies met with little opposition in restoring the old dynasties and régimes at the Vienna Congress – a suitable social infrastructure was already in place in the countries concerned.

## 3 Napoleon's Expectations from the Empire

Napoleon's expectations from the annexed territories and from the satellite states were, naturally enough, different. The annexed territories were treated as the rest of France. They enjoyed the same rights, and were subject to the same social and legal obligations, as well as the provision of conscripts and the payment of taxes.

The position of the satellite states was very different. They were never allowed to forget that they existed only to serve the interests of France. They not only formed a strategically important buffer zone (see page 56) to protect French borders, but fulfilled a number of other valuable functions in Napoleon's imperial enterprise. They were first and foremost military vassal states and Napoleon's relationship with them was eventually very like that of a medieval 'warrior over-lord', extracting the maximum advantage from them for the minimum return. They raised about a third of the total strength of the *Grande Armée* in the form of auxiliary troops, and were used to support and provision the regular army which continued in the Revolutionary tradition to 'live off the land' wherever it was garrisoned outside France. In addition, as the price of defeat, they had to pay substantial tribute monies which were used to finance Napoleon's future campaigns.

A good example of Napoleon's treatment of a satellite state is the Kingdom of Italy. The military and financial demands made on it in the interests of France ruined its economy. From 1806 onwards its six million inhabitants had to pay an annual tribute of one and a half million pounds to the French treasury, as well as making substantial cash contributions for such enterprises as ship-building. When the supply of currency ran out and the Viceroy protested that it was impossible for the kingdom, now heavily in debt, to continue supporting 100,000 French troops on its soil or to find any more ready money, Napoleon replied not with help but by adding to its obligations the outstanding debts of the Papal States, and by demanding a year later an extra million and a half pounds towards the cost of the campaign in Russia. The kingdom was also forced to recruit and maintain an army of 55,000 men for French service outside Italy. In addition to all this, the working of the Continental Blockade placed a severe strain on the commercial life of the country (see below, page 63) and destroyed its silk industry. The story in other satellite states was not dissimilar.

As well as their military and financial uses, the satellite states provided for Napoleon's dynastic and social needs. The distribution of crowns among Bonaparte relatives served two purposes for Napoleon. It enabled him to fulfil his clan loyalties (see page 5) to his brothers and sisters, with the expectation that in return they would remain loyal to him and so secure his hold over the Empire. Also, with such a large number of Bonaparte sovereigns available he could expect in due course to arrange useful marriage alliances with older royal houses and give his successors the dynastic respectability the family presently lacked.

When the Imperial nobility was created it became necessary to endow them with lands and revenues. The completeness of the Revolutionary land settlement left Napoleon with no suitable available land in France for these endowments, nor for rewarding lesser military or civilian personnel. The satellite states were used to provide the necessary land. Poland in particular was despoiled in this way, to the grave detriment of her economy. Even before the formal creation of the Grand Duchy of Warsaw, major endowments of land were made to 27 French marshals and generals. These gifts alone were on a scale which deprived the Duchy treasury of a fifth of its potential revenue from the former royal lands. The loss of income from further enormous land-gifts, added to other financial demands, ended by bankrupting the Duchy.

In a typical outburst Napoleon scolded his brother Louis, King of Holland for not putting France first at all times:

1 I myself drew up the constitution which was to provide the basis
  of your Majesty's throne on which I placed you. I hoped that
  developing in close proximity to France, Holland would possess
  that affection for France which the French nation has the right to
5 expect of its children, and even more so of its princes. I hoped
  that, raised in my political principles, you would feel that
  Holland, which has been conquered by my subjects, only owes its
  independence to their generosity; that Holland lacking allies and
  an army could be, and would deserve to be conquered on the day
10 it sets itself in opposition to France ... I have sufficient
  grievances against Holland to declare war on her.

In 1806 he spelled out just as clearly to Joseph the King of Naples the need to give priority to French interests:

1 I see that you promise in one of your proclamations not to impose

any war taxation and that you forbid Our soldiers to demand full
board from their hosts . . . these measures are too narowly
conceived. You do not win people to your side by cajoling them
5 . . . Levy a contribution of 30 millions from the kingdom of
Naples . . . it would be ridiculous if the conquest of Naples did
not bring comfort and wellbeing to My army.

Far from considering the happiness of the Neapolitans, Napoleon
continued the same letter with advice on the need to instil fear in order
to govern effectively and maintain the stability of the Empire:

1 If you do not make yourself feared from the beginning you are
bound to get into trouble . . . your proclamations do not make it
clear enough who is master. You will gain nothing by too many
caresses . . . if they [the people] detect they have no master over
5 them, they will turn to rebellion and mutiny.

In no context was the subservient position of the satellite states made
more obvious than in connection with the operation of the Continental
Blockade as a 'one-way common market'.


## 4  Effect of the Continental Blockade on the Empire

Historians are divided in their views on whether the annexed lands
benefited or not from Napoleon's control over their affairs. Some
consider it to have brought valuable material advantages in its wake
and, at least for a time, one of these advantages may well have been the
working of the Continental Blockade (see page 114) for part of its
purpose was to protect home markets against foreign competition.
Theoretically, home markets included those of the annexed territories.
This, however, was not entirely true. Piedmont, for instance, was as
greatly discriminated against as the Kingdom of Italy in the matter of
exporting silk. In order to increase production by the silk manufacturers of Lyon, Piedmont was prohibited from providing silk for manufacture anywhere else. As far as the satellite states were concerned, the
Blockade operated entirely to their disadvantage. Against them one-
sided preferential tariffs and equally one-sided trade restrictions were
imposed.

The Imperial decrees of 1806 and 1810, for instance, abolished the
traditional trading links between the Kingdom of Italy and her
neighbours. All export trade must be with France only; at the same
time Italy was 'reserved' as a market, or rather 'dumping ground', for
French goods of all kinds at high prices. Eugène de Beauharnais,
Viceroy of the Kingdom of Italy was threatened with annexation if his
country exported silk anywhere except to France:

1 It is no use for Italy to make plans that leave French prosperity
out of account. Above all she must be careful not to give France
any reason for annexing her; for if it paid France to do this, who
could stop her? So make this your motto too: France first (*la*
5 *France avant tout*).

Louis, King of Holland, received a warning about his slackness in
enforcing the Blockade:

1 . . . the independence of Holland can continue only so long as it is
not incompatible with the interests of France . . . Unless care is
taken to avoid thwarting the system of trade [the Continental
Blockade] laid down by France, Holland may lose her independ-
5 ence.

Apart from the manufacturing industries, Napoleon's economic
policy also had a blighting effect on farming communities in the satellite
states, especially in the good years when France produced enough food
of her own and there was nowhere else to which they were allowed to
send their surplus foodstuffs. This resulted in severely depressed
agricultural prices in much of the Empire, which in turn led to a lower
standard of living for those who could no longer afford the inflated
prices demanded for imported French goods, the only ones available for
purchase.

## 5 Napoleon's Motives for Creating the Empire

The official rationale for Napoleonic expansion was the continuing need
to protect the territorial integrity of Revolutionary France from attack
by the 'old monarchies' and the new need to export the Civil Code, the
Concordat and other benefits of Napoleonic rule to the oppressed
peoples of neighbouring states. This latter philanthropic mission would
produce a 'degree of liberty, equality and prosperity hitherto unknown'
outside France. It would ensure the end of the old régimes and 'provide
real guarantees to citizens everywhere in the Empire against arbitrary
government action', because government would be founded on 'principles which were noble, adapted to ideas of the individual country and
suited to the real needs of the people'. These praiseworthy aims were
the public face of Imperial expansion – less noble sentiments were
expressed more truthfully in private by Napoleon. To the kings of the
satellite states he wrote that they must establish the Civil Code because
'it will fortify your power, since by it all entails are cancelled and there
will no longer be any great estates except those you create yourselves.
This is the motive which has led me to recommend a civil code and its
establishment everywhere'.
Historians have argued interminably over what really drove Napo-

leon to create the Empire. As so often, in dealing with Napoleon, the situation is confused. It is difficult to determine from the evidence available, much of which is contradictory, which of his words and deeds were preplanned and which were spur of the moment affairs; which reflected his real policies and which were pragmatic compromises. As he himself said, 'I would often have been hard put to it to be able to assert with any degree of truth what was my whole and real intention'. Most historians would now agree that no single interpretation provides a complete answer to the question of Napoleon's motives. In the past 'overweening ambition', personal glory, and the pursuit of power for its own sake were commonly adjudged his guiding lights, but these now seem too simplistic explanations for such a complex personality. It is likely that there were other motives as well, forming a much more diverse pattern than was previously thought, and one in which different elements predominated at different times. One of these elements was undoubtedly his preoccupation with the idea of a universal empire. Another, and less credible, one was his alleged desire to encourage nationalism in the countries of the Empire.

## a) Universal Empire

In 1812 one of his advisers dared mention to Napoleon that 'the Great Powers are becoming afraid of a universal monarchy. Your dynasty is already spreading everywhere, and other dynasties fear to see it established in their own countries'. However, Napoleon was not annoyed, but was pleased with the information. A universal monarchy was the first step towards achieving his long-held dream of a universal empire made up of French-controlled vassal states.

Metternich, the Austrian Chancellor, certainly thought this dream was the basis of Napoleon's ambition. 'Napoleon's system of conquests was unique', he wrote. 'The object of universal domination to which he aspired was not the concentration of an enormous region in the immediate hands of the government, but the establishing of a central supremacy over the states of Europe, after the ideal . . . in the Empire of Charlemagne'. Support for Metternich's belief is to be found in Napoleon's quite extraordinary correspondence with the Pope between 1806 and 1808 which reveals his obsession with Charlemagne. The Holy Roman Emperor, still widely regarded as Charlemagne's titular successor, had been dispossessed by Napoleon, who, at least in his own mind, had taken his place when he crowned himself as King of Italy at Milan in May 1805:

1 As far as the Pope is concerned, I *am* Charlemagne. Like Charlemagne I join the crown of France with the iron crown of Lombardy, My Empire, like Charlemagne's, marches with the east. I therefore expect the Pope to accommodate his conduct to

5 my requirements. If he behaves well [i.e. implements the Continental Blockade] I shall make no outward changes – if not, I
shall reduce him to the status of a Bishop of Rome.

By 1808, having failed to come to an agreement with the Pope, he
took upon himself the right, as the new Charlemagne, to quash the
Donation of his predecessor, imprison the Pope and annex the Papal
States to the kingdom of Italy. (This Donation was the gift of Rome and
most of Italy to the Pope, and alleged to have been made by
Charlemagne to provide temporal as well as spiritual power for the
Church.)

At the height of his power (1811), Napoleon's Empire with its
satellite, family-ruled kingdoms exceeded the limits of Charlemagne's;
his son's title of King of Rome, formerly borne by the Habsburg heirs
to the Holy Roman Empire, underlined his Imperial power and
dynastic legitimacy. A number of historians believe that it was at this
point that Napoleon began to regard the Empire of Charlemagne as
merely a first stage in his ambitions, and to look to founding a new
Roman Empire as his future goal. This, given Napoleon's known
admiration for Caesar (and Alexander) as well as Charlemagne, his
interest in the East and his decision to make Rome the second city of his
Empire, is a possibility, but no more, for there is no real evidence to
substantiate the theory.

## b) Nationalism

In the accounts which he dictated on St Helena, Napoleon spoke about
the hopes he had entertained of fulfilling the national aspirations of his
subject peoples and of his sorrow that the machinations of the 'old
monarchies' had prevented him from doing so. Given time and peace,
he told Las Cases (see page 129), he would have been successful in a
programme of national unification:

1 One of my grandest ideas was *l'agglomération*; the concentration
of peoples geographically united, but separated by revolutions
and political action. There are scattered over Europe more than
30 million French, 15 million Spanish, 15 million Italians and 30
5 million Germans. My intention was to make each of these peoples
into a separate national state.
As regards the 15 million Italians, *l'agglomération* had already
gone far; it needed only time to mature; every day ripened that
unity of principles and legislation, of thought and of feeling,
10 which is the sure and infallible cement of human societies. The
annexation of Piedmont and Parma were only temporary expe-
dients; the single aim was to guide, guarantee and hasten the
national education of the Italian people.

A similar concern for Italian unity is credited to Napoleon by another of his St Helena companions:

1 Napoleon wanted to recreate Italy as a fatherland: to reunite the Venetians, the Milanese, the people of Piedmont, the Genoese, the Tuscans, the inhabitants of Parma and Modena, the Romans, the Neapolitans, Sicilians and Sardinians into a single indepen-
5 dent nation, frontiered by the Alps, the Adriatic, the Ionian Sea and the Mediterranean . . . Rome, the Eternal City would have been the capital of this state.

These declarations used to be taken at their face value and were repeated uncritically in numerous textbooks. Now they are more often ascribed to Napoleon's desire to liberalise his image (see pages 129–30 ) in the light of changing political circumstances after 1815. What ever he may have said after 1815, he never, while in power, tolerated nationalist ambitions among his subject peoples – or their rulers. He became meglomanic in his dealings with them, appearing in later years as the dictator who alone knew what was best for the Empire:

1 . . . my Italian subjects know me too well to forget that there is more in my little finger that in all their heads put together. In Paris where people are more enlightened than in Italy, they hold their tongues and bow to the judgement of a man who has proved
5 that he sees further and more clearly than they do. I am surprised that in Italy they are less obliging. (1806)

I understand Italian affairs better than anyone else. (1810)

When, in 1810, Holland was annexed to France Napoleon wrote:

1 I shall do what suits the interests of My Empire. I did not take over the government of Holland in order to consult the common people of Amsterdam or to do what they want. The French nation has been wise enough to rely upon my judgement. My hope is
5 that the Dutch will come to have the same opinion of me.

In Spain he so misjudged the situation that he expected to impose French rule there with little or no difficulty:

1 Some agitations may take place, but the good lesson which has just been given the city of Madrid [the massacre carried out by Murat in May 1808] will naturally soon settle affairs . . . The Spaniards are like other people and are not a class apart; they will
5 be happy to accept the imperial institutions.

The old beliefs that Napoleon was a reformer who consciously rationalised and systematised the conquered territories, socially, legally and economically, and so began the process of 'modernisation' in Germany and Italy, have now been considerably undermined (see page 59). It remains true, however, that by 1811, geographically speaking, he had much simplified the map of Europe by amalgamating and rearranging small states into larger blocks; but this was done without regard to national considerations. The new blocks were simply constructed as convenient administrative units for the Grand Empire. They were not intended to provide the basis for new 'nation-states'.

His universal Empire by its very nature was 'the negation of nationality'. How was it then that Napoleon came to be so firmly associated in older textbooks with paving the way for national unity, among the peoples of the Empire? That belief was based on Napoleon's own words about wanting to 'unify each of these peoples', words which are now generally discounted as no more than wishful thinking – just a part of the Legend. While he took no positive steps to encourage nationalism, in a negative way, the effect of his actions *was* to arouse nationalist ambitions in Germany and, to a lesser extent in Italy, Poland, Spain and Russia.

In the later eighteenth century, even before the French Revolution, philosophers were moving away from the cosmopolitan ideas of the Enlightenment and thinking seriously of nationalism as an important new force in contemporary politics: 'A kingdom consisting of a single nation is a family, a well-regulated household; it . . . is founded by nature and stands and falls by time alone. An empire, formed by forcing together a hundred nations and a hundred and fifty provinces, is no body politic, but a monster', at least according to one late eighteenth century German writer. The success of the Revolution in establishing during the 1790s a spirit of French unity and national solidarity encouraged nationalist murmurings elsewhere in Europe, where new importance was being attached to local customs and traditional culture, to shared national language and beliefs. Napoleonic imperialism gave a further impetus to nationalist developments by provoking a spirit of resistance to foreign, that is French, rule and to the military and financial burdens which accompanied it. Nowhere was this process more marked than in Germany, and most particularly in Prussia.

It happened that as the eighteenth century ended Germany was enjoying a great cultural renaissance in which music, philosophy and literature all played a part. The playwright Schiller defined the current mood when he wrote in 1802, 'The greatness of Germany consists in its culture and the character of the nation, which are independent of its political fate'. The catastrophic defeat of Prussia in 1806 changed the whole German situation. The process of Prussian recovery changed cultural self-satisfaction into political nationalism, which began with a strange mixture of adopting French ideas and reacting against French domination. Its development was unintentionally assisted by Napoleon when he defeated Austria and destroyed the Holy Roman Empire, weakening the political influence of the Habsburgs, which had always been a divisive one, and encouraging the Prussian ideas of leading a future united all-German state. With the dual aims of military reform and internal reorganisation, Prussia created a national army, and a strong central government, together with a new education system. All designed along French lines, they were intended to infuse into the people a common spirit of patriotic devotion to the cause of *German* nationalism. 'I know only one Fatherland and that is Germany' said one of the chief Prussian reformers; and in 1813 the Battle of Leipzig which drove out the French and destroyed the Confederation of the Rhine became a German patriotic legend.

In Italy the situation was different. There was none of the idea of a *Volk* there, a people bound together by a common heritage and shared language, as there was in Germany. Italian sentiment, too, was less generally anti-French than elsewhere. Indeed, the urban middle-class actively welcomed the reduction of Catholic power brought about by Napoleon's confrontations with the Pope. There was little or no public response during the Hundred Days to the proclamation issued by the flamboyant Murat, Napoleon's brother-in-law and King of Naples, declaring war on Austria and calling on all Italians to fight for national unity and independence. (His campaign was initially successful when he marched north and captured Rome and Bologna, but soon afterwards he was defeated by an Austrian army, and was later shot). The idea that Napoleon paved the way for Italian unification, and that his rule 'was a landmark in the history of the *Risorgimento*' (the Italian nineteenth-century nationalist movement) is only indirectly true. Italian national aspirations did not gain ground until *after* 1815, as a political reaction to the unwelcome restoration of most of the old ruling families and the old régimes.

Napoleon's part in the growth of Polish nationalism is a strange one. Poland, obliterated by her neighbours, Russia, Austria and Prussia between 1772 and 1795, was given a new, if partial, lease of life by Napoleon, when he created the satellite Grand Duchy of Warsaw in 1807 and gave it a new constitution. This was welcomed by the Poles with enormous enthusiasm as a step towards the full reinstatement of their country. Napoleon, however, ignored Polish nationalist ambitions and used the Duchy simply as a military vassal and a pawn in his dealings with Russia. In 1812 when he needed troops for the Russian campaign, he made actual if vague promises of future independence for the Poles in return for 98,000 men. The men were found but the promises were never fulfilled. Nevertheless, the Poles continued to support Napoleon to the bitter end, and for their pains lost everything. Poland was again divided among her neighbours at Vienna; but Polish nationalism did not die. It survived, based on Romantic traditions of military glory gained by her soldiers as a part of Napoleon's *Grande Armée* on battlefields all over Europe. These heroics sustained the Poles well into the twentieth century, during which time Napoleon, who treated them so cynically, continued to appear in art and literature as the focus for their dreams of national independence.

Russia and Spain are usually included in the list of countries where Napoleon's activities are claimed to have had some influence on the development of nationalism. However, although in both countries the people were temporarily united by hatred of the French invaders and by the savagery of the fighting, any lasting effects were in fact minimal.

The whole question of Napoleon's relationship with nationalism is a complicated one. As a young man he had seen and sympathised with the rise of nationalist sentiments in France at the Revolution. He spoke later about the 'great people' and their right to nationhood, but, what was right for his own people was not in his opinion the automatic right of others. It was 'France first and always', and the Empire must serve the interests of France. Did he not realise that sweeping away the old ruling dynasties of Europe and replacing them with an unwelcome foreign government would create, especially in Germany, the very thing he was trying to avoid, the growth of nationalist aspirations? Nationalism within the Empire was, though, largely the prerogative of the intellectual middle classes, and hardly touched the mass of the people, who had enough to do to keep themselves and their families alive without worrying about political ideals. It would be wrong, therefore, to consider the basically peasant armies of the Allies as fighting a war of 'national' liberation in 1813 as some historians have claimed. At the so-called 'Battle of the Nations' (Leipzig) they fought out of traditional loyalty to the Ancien Régime and to drive away the French, not for reasons of national pride.

## 6 Summary

Napoleon's Imperial policies were not altruistic. He had no intention of exporting the benefits of the Revolution to the rest of Europe, nor of fostering happiness among his peoples, nor of developing national unity in Germany, Italy or elsewhere. These things might happen as the result of Imperial expansion, but if they did, they were purely incidental to it, not the mainspring for it.

Was Napoleon's Empire founded on unbounded personal ambition, desire for military glory, a dictator's hunger for power, or the patriot's ambition to see France secure, pre-eminent in Europe, and the ideals of the Revolution safeguarded – or some combination of these? Was he motivated by the dream of universal empire, or driven by the need to fulfil the destiny he believed in? The questions are open ones – the answers must depend, as always in dealing with Napoleon, on individual interpretation of the facts as far as they can be known, weighing up the probabilities and analysing the evidence. Much hinges on the complexities of Napoleon's own character and it might be helpful to read through the remainder of this book before trying to decide what were the motives underlying the foundation of the Napoleonic Empire.

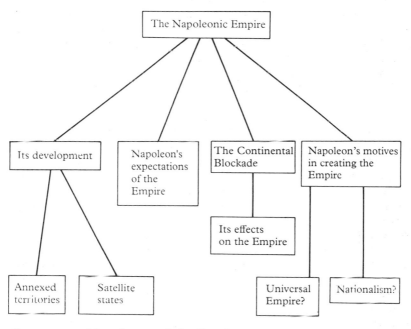

*Summary – Napoleon and the Empire*

---

### Making notes on 'Napoleon and the Empire'

This chapter deals in detail with the following aspects of the Napoleonic Empire: Napoleon's relations with the conquered territories (the annexed territories and the satellite states); the Continental Blockade and its effects on the Empire; Napoleon's reasons for creating the Empire and his attitude to nationalism within it.

You may find the headings given below helpful in making your notes. Afterwards you may wish to write brief answers to the accompanying questions:

1 The Development of the Empire
   (Refer to the map on page 26 and to the reference list of 'Territories of the Empire' (page 57). Make sure you appreciate the extent of the Empire.)

2 The Conquered Territories

(What were the differences between the Annexed Territories and Satellite States? Make sure you know which were which.)
3  Napoleon's Expectations from his Empire
   (What were they?)
4  The Continental Blockade
   (What were its effects on the Empire? Was its introduction a mistake by Napoleon?)
5  Napoleon's underlying motives for creating an empire.
   (Does it seem likely that he was motivated by the ideal of a universal empire? What was his attitude towards nationalism within the Empire? How far was he responsible for later nationalist developments in Italy and Germany?)

---

### Answering essay questions on 'Napoleon and the Empire'

Examination questions on Napoleon and the Empire tend to concentrate on one of two topics – the effects of the Continental Blockade and the growth of nationalism. The questions themselves take a wide variety of forms and vary considerably in difficulty and scope from the largely narrative to the mainly analytical. Look at the following examples. Which are the most difficult? which the easiest? why?
1  Is it true that the Berlin Decrees of 1806 marked a turning point in the fortunes of the Napoleonic Empire?
2  'The effects of Napoleon's Continental Blockade on the territories of the Empire were entirely disastrous'. Do you agree?
Questions may, however, include France as well as the Empire. The effects of the Blockade on France are dealt with in chapter 7, pages 113–116 and you may wish to wait until later before answering the next three questions:
3  Why and with what results did Napoleon establish his Continental Blockade?
4  Was the introduction of the Continental Blockade a serious mistake by Napoleon?
5  'Napoleon's Continental Blockade was doomed to failure from the start'. Is this view justified?
'Napoleon and nationalism' is usually dealt with by examiners in connection with the end of the Empire. For example:
6  To what extent was the final defeat of Napoleon due to the growth of nationalism within the Empire?
7  How far did Napoleon himself provoke nationalist hostility within the Empire against him?
8  How far is it true to say that Napoleon was finally overthrown by nationalist uprisings against him?

These last questions of the 'To what extent?' or 'How far?' type each require two-part answers. The first part sets out reasons for saying 'This far, or to this extent, yes', while the second part looks at reasons for saying 'This far, or to this extent, no'. The essay should finish with a paragraph setting out the conclusions (the relative strengths and weaknesses of the 'yes' and 'no' arguments) drawn from the information you have presented. Do not be put off by questions of this kind. The format is helpful for it suggests part of the answer. Question 6 for instance gives one reason for the final defeat of Napoleon. What were the other reasons?

---

*Source-based questions on 'Napoleon and the Empire'*

**1 The Satellite States**

Carefully read the series of short extracts on pages 60, 62, 63, 64, 65, 66 and 67. Answer the following questions.

a) Paraphrase in not more than three sentences Napoleon's advice on government contained in his letter to Eugène (page 60). How would you describe the advice? (*5 marks*)

b) In the letters to his brothers (pages 60, 62, 63 and 64) what attitude does Napoleon display towards them and the satellite states? Illustrate your answer with specific examples. What is the general tone of all the letters? Is it surprising? Explain your answer. (*6 marks*)

c) In the extracts on pages 62, 64 and 67 what is Napoleon's message to the satellite states? What was the penalty for ignoring it? (*4 marks*)

# CHAPTER 6

# Napoleon and France: Politics and Power

## 1 The Consolidation of Power

The successful conclusion of the *coup* was only the beginning for Napoleon. He had gained political power, but needed to consolidate it if he were to make himself undisputed ruler of France. He began with the constitution.

### a) The Constitution

Late in the evening of 19 Brumaire year VIII (10 November 1799) the three newly-elected provisional consuls (Napoleon, Sieyès and Ducos) swore an oath of allegiance to the Republic. At the same time Napoleon issued his first Proclamation:

> 1 On my return to France I found that the Constitution was half
>   destroyed and no longer capable of maintaining our liberty . . .
>   The Council of Ancients called on me – I answered the appeal . . .
>   I offered myself to the Five Hundred, my head uncovered, alone,
> 5 unarmed . . . twenty assassins rushed upon me, aiming at my
>   breast . . .

On the following day another proclamation, in the names of all three consuls this time, explained the need for the *coup*:

> 1 The Constitution of Year III (1795) was dying. It was incapable of
>   protecting your rights, even of protecting itself. Through repe-
>   ated assaults it was losing beyond recall the respect of nations.
>   Selfish factions were despoiling the republic. France was entering
> 5 the last stage of general disorganisation. But patriots have made
>   themselves heard. All who could harm you have been cast aside.
>   All who can serve you, all those representatives who have
>   remained pure have come together under the banner of liberty
>   . . . Frenchmen, the republic strengthened and restored to that
> 10 rank in Europe which should never have been lost, will realise all
>   the hopes of her citizens and will accomplish her glorious destiny.
>   Swear with us the oath which we have taken, to be faithful to the
>   republic, one and indivisible, founded on equality, liberty and the
>   representative system.

Within a few hours of the *coup* there were expressions of anxiety among the *philosophes* (liberal intellectuals interested in the general philosophy of government and society) particularly when it became known that under the Law of Brumaire the two legislative councils had been adjourned. On 20 Brumaire Benjamin Constant warned Sieyès that

1 This step appears disastrous to me in that it destroys the only
  barrier against a man with whom you associated yesterday but
  who is threatening the republic. His proclamations, in which he
  speaks only of himself and says that his return has given rise to
5 the hope that he will end France's troubles, have convinced me
  more than ever that in everything he does he sees only his own
  advancement.

In the Luxembourg Palace in Paris the consuls set to work on the new constitution, bypassing the two Standing Committees which were supposed to draw up the draft plans. In a series of long and often heated discussions Sieyès' proposals were gradually eroded by Napoleon's forceful arguments on his own behalf, and were eventually abandoned.

Sieyès had wanted two legislative councils, in addition to a senior body of senators, an executive consisting of two consuls (one in charge of foreign and the other of domestic affairs) and a 'Great Elector'. About the legislature and the senate there was little dispute; the question of the executive was another matter. It soon became clear that Sieyès, in a last ditch attempt to salvage his original plan for the *coup*, suggested that Napoleon should retire gracefully, becoming the purely nominal head of state, the Great Elector. With a large salary and little authority, he would live quietly at Versailles – 'wallowing there like a fatted pig' as Napoleon said angrily. He refused to countenance the idea. There must, he argued, be a First Consul as head of state, who would have complete control, in peace and in war, at home and abroad; and *he* must be that consul. The roles of the second and third consuls also caused argument. Sieyès wanted them each to have *voix deliberative* (the right to one of three equal votes). Napoleon insisted they should have only *voix consultative* (the right only to express an opinion). In all matters his decision would be final. Sieyès proved unable to withstand Napoleon's domineering personality and was eventually forced into the humiliating position of having to make the official nomination of Napoleon as First Consul. All three consuls would serve initially for ten years.

The negotiations had taken about six weeks to complete. In this time the government of France had been transformed from one where political responsibility was spread as widely as possible to one where it was centralised in the hands of a single man – a dictator.

Sieyès was compensated for the ruin of his plans and the loss of his hoped for consulship by being given the presidency of the Senate and a large estate in the country. 'Gentlemen, you have got yourselves a master', he is reported to have said of Napoleon at the end of the negotiations, 'a man who knows everything, wants everything, and can do everything'.

In a proclamation Napoleon explained to the French people his reasons for seizing power:

> To make the Republic loved by its own citizens, respected abroad and feared by its enemies – such are the duties we have assumed in accepting the First Consulship

and added reassuringly that the new constitution was

> based upon the true principles of representative government and on the sacred rights of property, equality and liberty. The powers it sets up will be strong and lasting.

But was this in fact the case? Was the constitution based on representative government? The electoral system adopted at the beginning of the consulate was Sieyès' invention and certainly provided for 'universal suffrage', unlike the property-based vote of the 1795 constitution. But this suffrage was so indirect as to be of little significance in relation to the idea of popular sovereignty (that is, the idea that the people should exercise control over their government, usually by directly electing a representative assembly). There were, it is estimated, about six million 'Frenchmen of the age of 21 with a year's domicile' named as voters on the commune registers in 1799. These six million men chose 10 per cent of their number to form a communal list (from whom local officials would be drawn), and that was the end of the direct vote. These 600,000 in turn chose 10 per cent of their number to form a departmental list, and these finally chose 6,000 of themselves to go on to a national list of 'persons fit for public service'. From this national list of 'notables' the Senate chose the members of the two legislative bodies – the Tribunate of 100 members aged 25 or more who could discuss legislation but could not vote on it, and a Legislature of 300 members aged 30 or more who could vote on legislation by secret ballot but could not discuss it. The Senate (some 60 distinguished men aged 40 or more, and holding office for life) was itself nominated by the First Consul, who also presided over the Council of State of 30 to 40 men, who were chosen by him. The Council nominated all major central and local government officials, and initiated all legislation.

The references to a constitution based on representative government were merely words. Democratic involvement in the elections was minimal. While there was the appearance of adult male suffrage, there were no *elections*, only *presentations* of candidates suitable for appointment as deputies, and the choice of candidates was restricted to

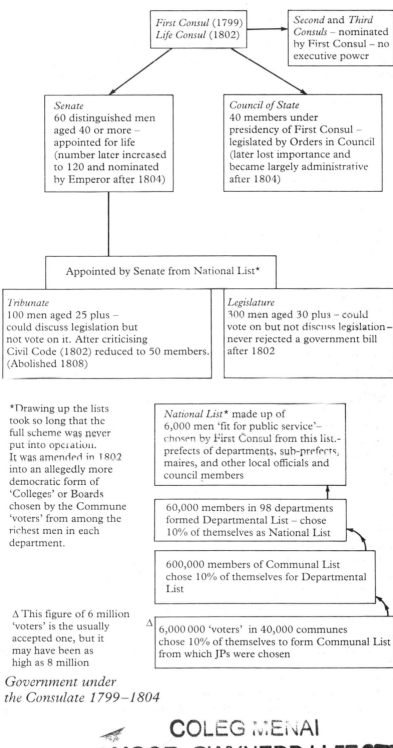

**First Consul** (1799)
**Life Consul** (1802)

**Second** and **Third Consuls** – nominated by First Consul – no executive power

**Senate**
60 distinguished men aged 40 or more – appointed for life (number later increased to 120 and nominated by Emperor after 1804)

**Council of State**
40 members under presidency of First Consul – legislated by Orders in Council (later lost importance and became largely administrative after 1804)

Appointed by Senate from National List*

**Tribunate**
100 men aged 25 plus – could discuss legislation but not vote on it. After criticising Civil Code (1802) reduced to 50 members. (Abolished 1808)

**Legislature**
300 men aged 30 plus – could vote on but not discuss legislation – never rejected a government bill after 1802

*Drawing up the lists took so long that the full scheme was never put into operation. It was amended in 1802 into an allegedly more democratic form of 'Colleges' or Boards chosen by the Commune 'voters' from among the richest men in each department.

**National List*** made up of 6,000 men 'fit for public service'– chosen by First Consul from this list.– prefects of departments, sub-prefects, maires, and other local officials and council members

60,000 members in 98 departments formed Departmental List – chose 10% of themselves as National List

600,000 members of Communal List chose 10% of themselves for Departmental List

Δ This figure of 6 million 'voters' is the usually accepted one, but it may have been as high as 8 million

Δ 6,000 000 'voters' in 40,000 communes chose 10% of themselves to form Communal List from which JPs were chosen

*Government under the Consulate 1799–1804*

notables – men of wealth, usually landowners or existing government officials.

Power was firmly in the hands of one man (the First Consul), who stood alone at the top of the political pyramid. He controlled government appointments, made and unmade ministers whom he closely supervised and to whom he allowed no freedom of action, initiated all legislation through the Council of State or the Senate, declared war and made peace. The Senate which had been intended by Sieyès to act as a brake on the executive, became under Napoleon's leadership an instrument of his personal power. The Senate was supposed to be the guardian of the existing constitution, but was also able to amend it by a legal procedure known as *senatus-consultum*. It was this procedure that Napoleon used extensively from January 1801 onwards in order to thwart the wishes of the Tribunate and the Legislature. Appointed for life, with a substantial salary and suitably rewarded with gifts of land and money, the Senators enjoyed considerable prestige. Membership of the Senate increased from the original 80 to about 140 by 1814, most of the extra members being Napoleon's direct nominees or *ex officio* 'grand dignatories' of the Empire, used to pack the Senate. As a result it developed into a largely consultative body anxious to please its benefactor and president, Napoleon.

Under the Law of Brumaire the new constitution, in order to become legal, had to be 'submitted to the acceptance of the French people'. In February 1800 a plebiscite was held and the electors were given a month in which to vote in their communes for or against the constitution. The official results showed 3,011,007 voting in favour with 1,562 against. This was not quite as overwhelming a display of public approval as the figures suggest. Voting took place at different times in different places, and the ballot was not a secret one. Voters simply wrote 'yes' or 'no' against their names on an open list. Not surprisingly, malpractice and intimidation affected the results in some areas. The government, made aware of the problem of possible later victimisation, promised to burn all lists when the votes had been counted. However, this promise was not kept and in many parts of France the lists are still available for study, providing useful evidence for social historians.

As the constitution had already been put (illegally) into operation, there was very little point in voting 'no', especially as many people feared that to do so might lead to trouble afterwards. Although a favourable vote would merely ratify a *fait accompli*, it was important to the government's credibility that the constitution should seem to be as widely accepted as possible. There is little doubt that before the voting figures were published they were adjusted by Lucien as Minister of the Interior in order to ensure a large majority for the government. He almost doubled the total number of 'yes' votes, rounding up the figures by about 900,000 and then adding in another 500,000 to represent the unanimously favourable votes it was alleged that the army would have cast if they had been included in the plebiscite. The real 'yes' vote was, therefore, probably only about 1,500,000. In addition, recent research has suggested that the number of those eligible to vote in the communes was probably much nearer 8,000,000 than the figure of 6,000,000 previously accepted by historians. The 'yes' votes therefore represented not something over 50 per cent of the electorate as once appeared, but only something under 20 per cent. Even if it were argued that the large number of abstentions ought to be considered as 'not opposed' and, thus, at least passively favourable to the new régime, it is difficult to accept the view of many historians that public opinion *was* sufficiently well inclined towards Napoleon and the new constitution at the beginning of 1800 to justify him regarding the result as a vote of confidence. The results of the plebiscite would appear to indicate public apathy rather than anything else.

It took a long time to draw up the massive communal, departmental and national lists, and the whole 'electoral' system proved extremely cumbersome when it was eventually put into operation in 1801. This was so much so that Napoleon abolished the system the following year even before all the lists were complete. He introduced a new arrangement which lasted until the end of the Empire and which reduced still further the element of popular choice. It was intended to produce groups of people who would act as intermediaries between government and people, (not between people and government as the previous arrangement had, however inadequately, tried to do). All adult males met to elect life members to departmental 'colleges', or boards. However, the electors had only a limited choice of candidates, for these life members had to be selected from a list of the 600 most heavily taxed and therefore the richest men in the department. Every five years the colleges produced lists of candidates for election to vacancies on the legislative bodies but their main function was to provide readily available groups of wealthy property owners (notables) for Napoleon to court with offers of central or local government posts or other benefits. In return for these favours he expected them to bring their wealth and influence to bear on behalf of the régime. It was an arrangement by which Napoleon not only rewarded the property owning classes for past support but also secured their loyalty for the future. It was to remain a favourite political manoeuvre until his final defeat.

## b) The Hereditary Principle

Napoleon only narrowly escaped assassination in December 1800, making the Senate anxiously aware of the fragile nature of a régime dependant for its continuation upon one man. Partly because of this, and partly as a demonstration of gratitude to the First Consul for his achievements at home and abroad, it was decided to offer him the Consulship for life, with the right to nominate his successor. It was the successor. It was the first step towards the re-introduction of hereditary rule. Napoleon accepted 'if the will of the people demands it', and so another plebiscite was held. The result was similar to that of 1799, (an alleged 3,600,000 in favour of making Napoleon Life Consul and 8,374 against). It is interesting to note that 40 per cent of the 'no' votes came from the army, which had been allowed to take part in the plebiscite this time. While there is no evidence that the central government tampered directly with the figures, it is known that local officials often sent in results which they thought would be pleasing to their superiors, sometimes even recording a unanimous 'yes' vote when, in fact, no poll at all had been held.

In his speech of thanks to the Senate for his appointment to the Life Consulship, Napoleon remarked that much still remained to be done to strengthen the constitution. One thing which was done almost immediately was to increase Napoleon's personal power through his control of an enlarged Senate, which became responsible for 'everything not provided for by the constitution, and necessary to its working'. This arrangement was greatly to the detriment of the representative bodies, the Tribunate and the Legislature. They lost much of their importance, and met more and more infrequently. The Tribunate was severely purged in 1802 for daring to criticise the Civil Code (see page 84) and with a much reduced membership became little more than a rubber stamp for the remainder of its existence (see page 81), while the Legislature's credibility was reduced by being 'packed' by Napoleon with 'safe' men who would not oppose his wishes.

By 1803 Napoleon was riding in splendour around Paris and holding court in royal style. State ceremonies multiplied, etiquette was formalised, official dress became more elaborate. The Legion of Honour (see page 83) had been introduced the previous year and there were hints that a nobility was to be re-established, the rumours fired by Napoleon's permission for a large number of *emigrés* to return to France. In 1804 a series of disasters, royalist plots and counter-plots culminated in the affair of the Duc d'Enghien, a member of the Bourbon royal family alleged to be involved in a plot to supplant Napoleon by murdering him and taking over the government. The Duke was kidnapped by Napoleon's orders while on neutral territory, tried and, on very inadequate evidence, found guilty of conspiracy. He was quickly executed in what amounted to judicial murder, justified by Napoleon on the grounds that he was entitled by the Corsican laws of vendetta to kill an enemy who threatened his personal safety. In the wake of these events Napoleon began to prepare the people for his next step:

The great number of plots which are woven against my life inspire no fear in me. But I cannot deny a deep feeling of distress when I consider the situation in which the great people would have found itself today had the recent attempt [at assasination] succeeded.

Others apart from Napoleon were considering what would happen to France if he should be murdered. The property-owners took seriously the Bourbon pretender's recent threat to return all 'stolen properties' to their 'rightful owners' as soon as he regained the throne, and most were convinced that only Napoleon stood between them and the loss of all they had gained by the Revolution. There was widespread talk of making the Consulship hereditary in the Bonaparte family, in the hope of providing for a smooth succession and the survival of the constitution should Napoleon meet an untimely death. Then, in May 1804, a formal motion was approved by the Senate that 'Napoleon Bonaparte at present First Consul be declared Emperor of the French, and that the imperial dignity be declared hereditary in his family'.

A third plebiscite was held in November 1804 asking the people whether they agreed that 'the hereditary and imperial dignity should descend through the direct natural, legitimate and adoptive heirs of Napoleon Bonaparte and the direct natural and legitimate heirs of Joseph Bonaparte and of Louis Bonaparte' (Lucien and Jérôme were pointedly excluded by Napoleon from the succession because he considered their wives to be unsuitable). The wording of the plebiscite was chosen to overcome the difficulty that Napoleon and his wife Josephine had no children, but to allow for a successor to come from within the Bonaparte family – an important point for a Corsican (see page 5). The plebiscite achieved the desired result (3,572,329 'yes' and 2,569 'no' votes). Remembering the adverse army vote two years earlier, the government took no chances this time and did not actually poll the soldiers. They simply added in about half a million 'yes' votes on their behalf.

At a sumptuous ceremony in the cathedral of Notre Dame in Paris held in the presence of the Pope, Napoleon, as previously arranged, took the imperial crown and placed it on his own head, before himself crowning Josephine as Empress. In his coronation oath Napoleon swore:

1 to uphold the integrity of the Republic's territory, to respect and impose the laws of the Concordat (see page 90) and the laws of equal rights, political and civil liberties, the irrevocability of the sale of national property, to raise no duty and establish no tax
5 except through the law, to uphold the institution of the Legion of Honour, and to rule only in the interests of the happiness and glory of the French people.

During the next two or three years the Tribunate and the Legislature were hardly consulted at all. The Tribunate was finally abolished in 1808 and, although the Legislature survived, it was only able to do so by maintaining its subservient attitude to Napoleon's demands. Government was increasingly conducted through the Senate and the

Council of State, both of which were firmly under Napoleon's personal control. In theory the Senate acquired important new powers in 1804 with the formation of two standing committees, one concerned with preserving individual liberty and the other with safeguarding freedom of the press. In fact, from the outset these committees were rendered impotent by Napoleon. Neither was allowed any real opportunity to consider complaints, and only a handful of cases were dealt with in ten years. The committee on freedom of the press was further handicapped by being debarred from considering anything connected with the publication of newspapers or periodicals!

Only one thing more was needed to establish the Napoleonic dynasty beyond question – the production of a legitimate son and heir. Napoleon went about it in his usual determined way. Despite his continued fondness for her, Josephine, now past child-bearing age, would have to be divorced, and a new wife selected; but first the Church had to be persuaded that Josephine should be set aside. This was not easy, for although their original marriage had been a civil one, the Church had insisted on a second, Catholic ceremony as a necessary preliminary to the coronation in 1804. Eventually, on the grounds of alleged irregularities in the conduct of the religious marriage, the Church agreed unwillingly to an annulment, leaving Napoleon free to remarry. A list of 18 eligible princesses was drawn up for him. In 1810, at the age of 40, he married the young Marie-Louise of Austria, a niece of the 'Austrian woman', Marie-Antoinette (Louis XVI's wife who had been executed during the Revolution). In the following year the hoped for son, Napoleon, King of Rome, was born. The succession seemed assured, the dynasty secure. 'I am at the summit of my happiness' Napoleon is reported to have said.

## 2  Maintaining Power

One of the first needs of the new government was money – there were only a few thousand francs in the Treasury in November 1799. In January 1800 the Bank of France was founded. At first it was a private venture, but it came under state control in 1806 and did much to establish the creditworthiness of the state. Also in 1800 the Treasury itself was reorganised to oversee the receipt, transfer and payment of state funds, and to audit state finances. A new and much more complete tax register was introduced for most of the country and the collection of direct taxes on land, personal income, and industrial profits was greatly improved through the development of a centralised hierarchy of tax-collectors working under the control of the Ministry of Finances in Paris. With the additional revenue from indirect taxes on consumer goods (the *droits réunis*) and from customs and other duties, by 1802 the state could meet its obligations on salaries and pensions, and government bonds rose in value. Napoleon had a hatred of paper money – the *assignats* of the early 1790s had been a disaster – and in 1803 he introduced a new metal coinage based primarily on a silver franc to replace earlier debased issues and to provide France with a strong and stable currency. As the result of these financial measures the country was solvent. Not until military expenditure began to outstrip available income in the years after 1806 did the financial situation deteriorate into annual deficit. However, before that happened Napoleon had acquired a stranglehold on power by pursuing a policy of uniformity and centralisation which brought all aspects of French life under his personal control.

## a) By Buying Support

Napoleon continued to cosset the property-owners and would-be property-owners throughout his time in power. He used gifts of money, land, titles, honours and government appointments to build up a strong body of personal support for himself, bind men to his service and ensure loyalty to his régime, particularly among the military.

In the 12 years following the establishment of the Legion of Honour in 1802 38,000 awards (only 4000 of which went to civilians) were made. However, although the decoration was prestigious, it carried no financial advantages, unlike the titles dreamt up for the officials of the new imperial court. These new titles, created between 1804 and 1808, ranged from 'grand dignataries' such as the arch-chancellor, through 'grand officers', down to lesser dignataries such as the prefects of the palace. Some of these titles brought with them large estates, and although these at first went only to members of the Bonaparte family, they were soon being bestowed on court officials and statesmen, as well as on the 18 outstanding generals who were created Marshals of France. The estates awarded to these generals were mostly in Poland, Germany and Italy. It was therefore probable that Napoleon's intention was to appeal to these men's self-interest to his own advantage. They knew that the only way of retaining their property was to remain loyal to Napoleon in the hope of maintaining the Empire's frontiers.

In 1808 Napoleon went further and began the creation of a whole new imperial nobility. All 'grand dignataries' became princes, archbishops became counts, mayors of large towns became barons, and members of the Legion of Honour were allowed to call themselves Chevaliers. These titles were awarded directly by the Emperor for state service, usually of a military kind. If the recipient possessed a large enough annual income – 200,000 francs in the case of a duke for instance – the titles could be made hereditary. Where worthy candidates for ennoblement had insufficient personal fortunes to support a title they were provided, like the generals, with fiefs in far-off parts of the Empire from which to raise the necessary revenue. In all, about 3,500 titles were granted between 1808 and 1814. One area in which civilians benefited was in the allocation of *senatoreries*. These were grants of large country estates to members of the Senate, together with a palatial residence and an annual income of 25,000 francs to support it. Included in the grant was appointment as *préfet* (prefect) (see page 86) not just of the usual *département* but of a whole region. Lesser individuals also benefited from Napoleon's personal gifts. For instance, more than 5000 presents of enough money to buy a house in Paris and to live there in comfort were made to army officers, government officials and minor members of the new nobility.

However, Napoleon seems to have realised from the beginning that bribery as a means of control was unreliable, and was not in itself enough to maintain popular support even among the recipients. Therefore, compulsion, intimidation and indoctrination all became part of the Napoleonic system of government.

## b) By Restricting Liberty

The restriction of individual liberty of thought, word and deed was an important element in Napoleon's autocratic government. By numerous measures, some more subtle than others, he built up over the years a system of supervision and control worthy of a modern dictator.

### i) The police
In European usage the word 'police' covers the entire system of rules and regulations for the maintenance of public order and state security, as well as the people entrusted with their administration and operation. Napoleon's police system was an important part of his centralised administration.

A number of changes were made to the judiciary. Judges, apart from local justices of the peace, instead of being elected as under the Directory, were appointed by the government for life and were kept subservient and loyal by a combination of close supervision and a system of 'purges'. A whole new hierarchy of judicial tribunals was set up.

The basis of the legal system, the Civil Code of 1804, later known as the *Code Napoléon*, was founded on the work of successive Revolutionary governments which had tried to organise some sort of acceptable nationwide legal system out of the conflicting customary laws of the north and the Roman law of the south. The early 1790s had seen a bias towards a system based on the liberal customary law with its acceptance of the equality of persons, civil marriage, divorce and the equal division of property between heirs; but from 1795 there had been a reaction in favour of the more authoritarian Roman law (a heritage from the days of the Roman Empire) which emphasised male authority and the father's rights. The Civil Code was strongly influenced by the precepts of Roman law – they accorded well with Napoleon's own views on society and the inferior status of women – and although it was the work of professional lawyers, Napoleon himself took a very active interest in its formulation, presiding personally over nearly half the sessions of the Senate which were devoted to its discussion. It has been praised by numerous historians as an important reform for its clear and understandable exposition of the law, but the Code itself was in many ways illiberal and restrictive in outlook, even by the standards of the day. Individual male rights to ownership of property were maintained and the civil rights of Frenchmen were assured, but married women fared badly under its double standards. A man had total authority over his wife and family – he could send an adulterous wife or defiant child to prison – and divorce, although permitted in theory, was made very difficult and expensive to obtain. There was a lack of liberty too in the treatment of negroes and workers. Slavery was reintroduced in the French colonies 'in accordance with the laws current in 1789', and workmen were made subject to close police supervision through use of the *livret*, a combined workpermit and employment record, without which it was impossible legally to obtain a job. The Code did, however, give legal sanction to some of the important developments of the 1790s – confirming the abolition of feudalism, and giving fixed legal title to those who had earlier purchased confiscated church, crown and emigré property (the *biens nationaux*). It also followed the Revolutionary principle of *partage*, that is, equal division of estates among male heirs instead of primogeniture.

The Civil Code was only the beginning and the Criminal, Commercial and Penal Codes which followed it were an attempt to codify the rest of French law in the same sort of way. The Criminal and Penal Codes were essentially concerned with punishment – perpetual hard labour, loss of the right hand and branding were among the penalties laid down. Special new courts proliferated – there were military courts, and tribunals for political offenders presided over by 'magistrates for public security'. In 1810 a system of arbitrary imprisonment without trial (similar to the *lettres de cachet* used in pre-revolutionary France) was reintroduced, although it was never extensively used, a form of house arrest being more usual (see page 86). A number of extra prisons were built and, although figures are difficult to come by, it is estimated that in 1814 they were occupied by about 16,000 ordinary convicts (more than three times as many as in 1800).

The general police, operating under the control of the Minister of Police (Fouché, for much of the Napoleonic era) had very wide ranging powers. In Paris they were employed to monitor the state of public opinion in the city and to report daily on variations in food prices.

1 Today everyone is very concerned about Spain and what is going on there. As usual it is all exaggerated. The Ministry of Police has taken measures to quash false rumours. People are no longer

complaining about the high price of coffee and sugar; many
5 people go without them.

In their capacity as trained spies they acted in connection with the
imposition of censorship, the surveillance of possible subversives, the
search for army deserters and the organisation of raids on areas believed
to be sheltering draft dodgers or enemy agents. They were assisted in
their more mundane police duties such as the maintenance of law and
order by the well-organised body of gendarmes, of whom there were
about 18,000 stationed throughout France in 1810. Reports were
submitted to Napoleon daily by Fouché on the work of his department,
but Napoleon also had other sources of information. He had a spy
network of his own, operating independently of Fouché, a secret police
whose activities caused considerable public anxiety. Letters were
opened, reports made, reputations destroyed, and careers blighted as
the result of information collected for Napoleon by these men – but not
only by them. A wide variety of provincial officials were expected to act
as spies in the course of their work, and to relay their findings back to
Paris.

The prefects (*préfets*) of *départements* or sub-prefects (*sous-préfets*) of
the *arrondissements* making up each department acted as agents of the
central government and were directly appointed by Napoleon. So too
were the members of their advisory councils, and the mayors (*maires*) of
the larger communes. The other mayors and all the municipal councils
were nominated by the prefect. The result was a highly centralised
bureaucracy for the collection of taxes, the enforcement of conscription, the dissemination of propaganda, and the obtaining of information, operating through a body of well-trained and loyal administrators.
The prefects, in particular, were expected to monitor public opinion in
their areas and to report on any suspicious political activity. A system of
house arrest was available through the prefects for anyone who did not
warrant imprisonment but who was considered a danger to state
security.

Not very different were the obligations laid on senators when
proceeding to their *senatoreries*. Napoleon wrote to them at length:

1 . . . Your most important duty will be to supply Us with trustwor-
thy and positive information on any point which may interest the
government, and to this end, you will send Us a direct report,
once a week . . . You will realise that complete secrecy must be
5 observed as this is a confidential mission . . . You will draw up
detailed returns of all information about these persons [public
officials, the clergy, teachers, men of importance, farmers, indus-
trialists, criminals] basing your information upon facts and send
the reports in to Us. You will observe the condition of the roads
10 . . . and investigate the state of public opinion on (i) the govern-

ment (ii) religion (iii) conscription (iv) direct and indirect taxation . . .

With such well-organised surveillance it is not surprising that the
régime met with little serious political opposition, especially as its
potential leaders, notables, intellectuals and members of the
bourgeoise, were increasingly tempted into allying themselves with the
government in the hope of rewards. The only means of opposition open
to the ordinary people were resisting conscription, deserting once
enlisted (despite the ferocious penalties it incurred) or joining one of the
bands of brigands which operated on a grand scale in much of the
French countryside. Conscription had always been unpopular ever
since it was introduced in 1793, but recent research shows that, until
the massive levies of 1813, resistance to it was much less under
Napoleon than it had been under the Directory. Over 90 per cent of the
expected levies were raised without difficulty in the years before 1808.
It may have been partly due to better administration, but while
Napoleon was winning victories and casualties were low, resistance to
conscription was not a serious problem. Only when the military tide
turned against him and the casualties mounted did it become so.

## ii) Censorship and Propaganda

The press was expected to act as the unquestioning mouthpiece of the
government and to be the purveyor of official propaganda. Napoleon
wrote

1 The newspapers are always ready to seize on anything which
  might undermine public tranquility . . . Newspapers . . .
  announce and prepare revolutions and in the end make them
  indispensable. With a smaller number of newspapers it is easier to
5 supervise them and to direct them more firmly towards the
  strengthening of the constitutional régime . . . I will never allow
  the newspapers to say or do anything against my interest.

In January 1800 he arbitrarily reduced the number of political
journals published in Paris from 73 to 13 and forbade the production of
any new ones. By the end of the year only nine remained. These
survivors were kept short of reliable news and were forbidden to discuss
controversial subjects. Their editors were forced to rely for news on the
military bulletins or longer political articles published in *Le Moniteur*,
the official government journal. These were written by Napoleon
himself or by his ministers, and 'to lie like a bulletin' soon became a
common saying (see page 127). In 1809 censors were appointed to each
newspaper and a year later provincial papers were reduced to one per
department. In 1811 all except four of the Parisian papers were

suppressed and those that remained were made subject to police supervision.

It was not only newspapers which were censored. Up to 1810 reports on all books, plays, lectures and posters which appeared in Paris were sent, often daily, to Napoleon, and publishers were required to forward two copies of every book, prior to publication, to police headquarters. In 1810 a regular system of censors was set up, more than half the printing presses in Paris were shut down, and publishers were forced to take out a licence and to swear an oath of loyalty to the government. Booksellers were strictly controlled and severely punished, even with death, if found to be selling material considered subversive. Authors were harassed and sometimes forced into exile if they criticised the government however slightly, while dramatists were forbidden to mention any historical event which might, however indirectly, reflect adversely on the present régime. Many theatres were closed down. Others operated only under licence and were restricted to putting on a small repertory of officially sanctioned plays. One poet was consigned to detention in a mental asylum for composing the couplet: 'The great Napoleon Is a great chameleon', not because of its feebleness, but because of its sentiments! The same fate awaited any priest who spoke disparagingly of Napoleon from the pulpit. Artists, sculptors and architects got off more lightly – dictators always need the publicity offered by buildings, statues and pictures, the larger the better. Napoleon became a substantial spender on arches, pillars and monuments on the grand scale, but also, it is only fair to add, a judicious patron of the decorative arts in a style which still bears the name of 'Empire'. Fashionable artists such as David (see the illustration on page 125) and Ingres (see cover portrait) were employed by Napoleon as state propagandists, depicting him as a romantic hero-figure, or the embodiment of supreme imperial authority in classical guise, often complete with toga and laurel wreath. David as 'painter to the government' was given the oversight of all paintings done in France, with particular reference to the suitability of the subject matter.

### iii) Education

Napoleon's interest in education was as a means of providing for state service not only loyal and disciplined army officers, but also well-trained civilian officials and administrators, all recruited from among the sons of the property-owning classes. Education for the common people was neglected by Napoleon, as it had been by the governments of the Ancien Régime and of the Revolution. A simple 'moral education' of an elementary nature was seen as being sufficient for them and was provided in primary schools run by the Church, by the local community or by individuals. Napoleon often declared his belief in equal opportunities for all according to ability and irrespective of birth or wealth, what he called 'careers open to talents', but he generally failed to ensure that this was carried out in practice. Secondary education was almost entirely restricted to the sons of *notables* who were educated, often free of charge if their fathers were army officers, in the 39 highly selective, militarised *lycées* first introduced in 1802, and to a lesser extent to boys attending the rather less high-powered secondary schools established three years later. No similar provision was made for the education of girls. Napoleon had a poor view of women, who 'should not be regarded as the equals of men; they are, in fact, mere machines to make children. I do not think we need bother about the education of girls ... Marriage is their destiny'. They did not, therefore, need to think and should not be taught to do so. Scientific study and research was also neglected after the *Polytechnique*, founded during the Revolution, was converted into a military academy in 1805.

In order to ensure that his wishes concerning education were complied with, Napoleon founded the Imperial University in 1808. This was not a university in the ordinary sense, but a kind of Ministry of Education developed from Napoleon's earlier 'Order of Teachers' and invested 'with sole responsibility for teaching and education throughout the Empire'. As Napoleon told the Council of State:

1 Of all our institutions education is the most important. It is essential that the morals and the political ideas of the generation which is now growing up should no longer be dependent on the news of the day or the circumstances of the moment. We must
5 secure unity; we must be able to cast a whole generation in the same mould. There will be no stability in the state until there is a body of teachers with fixed principles. Let us have a body of doctrine which does not vary and a body of teachers which does not die.

The University controlled the curricula and appointed all the teachers of the state secondary schools, which operated only by its permission and under its authority. Total obedience was demanded by the University from its member teachers, who had to take an oath of loyalty to their superiors, and were bedevilled by petty restrictions – a visit to Paris without special permission, for instance, would mean a spell in prison. Lessons were standardised, and what was taught was dictated in accordance with the needs and demands of the government.

There was no room for freedom of choice within the state system, nor for freedom of thought or expression by pupils or staff. For this reason many parents preferred to send their children, if they could, to the more expensive private Church schools especially when these became more easily available after the Concordat with the Pope in 1801.

*iv) Religion*
As early as the summer of 1800 Napoleon was making proposals for what used to be regarded by historians as the 'restoration' of the Catholic Church in France. However, the significance of this has been reduced by recent research which has shown that, as a result of the efforts of ordinary men and women during the time of the Directory, many parish churches had already been reopened and priests persuaded to officiate. It has convincingly been claimed that 'a Church was re-established from below long before the Concordat' which 'represented the recognition of a *fait accompli*'. It seems probable that matters had gone so far in the revival of Catholic public worship that no government could safely have ignored or opposed it, and that Napoleon's motives for seeking a *rapprochement* with the Pope were those of expediency.

Napoleon had been born and brought up a Catholic but, as a good Jacobin, he had become if not exactly an atheist at least an agnostic. Although the Napoleonic Legend was to have him die in the Catholic faith, he paid it no more than lip service during his adult life, and that only so that his coronation could follow the imperial tradition of Charlemagne. However, he appreciated the power of religion to act as the 'social cement' welding together a divided people, and the importance of its official re-establishment in bringing an end to the schism between clergy who had sworn allegiance to the Revolution and those who had not. Religious peace would help bring political and social peace to France. His opinion was that

1 No society can exist without inequality of fortunes; and inequality of fortunes cannot exist without religion. When a man is dying of hunger beside another who is stuffing himself with food, he cannot accept this difference if there is not an authority who tells
5 him, 'God wishes it so' . . . It is religion alone that gives to the state a firm and durable support.

Catholicism had become identified with the royalist cause. It needed instead to be identified with the people as a whole. If it could then be reunited with the state, loyal in its support of the head of state and under his control, it would be a force for peace and stability in the country, and draw Catholics away from their Bourbon allegiance.

Having decided that 'the people need a religion', Napoleon set about 'rebuilding the altars', but with the proviso that 'this religion must be in the hands of the government'. The Concordat between Napoleon and Pope Pius VII in 1801 was finally agreed on that basis. The Church recognised the Revolution and agreed that no attempt would be made to recover church lands. A state-controlled Church was established, and its clergy became paid civil servants, appointed by the government and bound to it by oath. While it was agreed that Catholic worship, 'the religion of the great majority of the citizens', should be 'freely exercised in France' it was also agreed that public worship should be 'in conformity with police regulations which the government shall deem necessary for public peace'. The Concordat was published by Napoleon in April 1802 as part of a wide ranging ecclesiastical law on to which he tacked the so-called 'Organic Articles'. These were a series of articles limiting in every possible way Papal control over the French bishops, and increasing with equal thoroughness state control over the activities of the clergy as a whole. 'The Head of the Church', Napoleon announced, 'has in his wisdom and in the interests of the Church considered proposals dictated by the interests of the state . . . What he has approved the government has listened to, and the legislature has made a law of the Republic'. He went to exhort the clergy:

1 See that this religion attaches you to the interests of the country.
  See that your teaching and your example shape young citizens in
  respect and affection for the authorities which have been created
  to protect and guide them. See that they learn from you that the
5 God of Peace is also the God of War, and that He fights on the
  side of those who defend the independence and liberty of France.

In 1806 Napoleon went a step further. By standardising the numerous existing church catechisms, he could turn a necessary ecclesiastical reform to political ends. The questions and answers of the new official catechism, as amended by Napoleon personally was taught in all schools and carried a very clear message, one that was not at all agreeable to the Pope:

1 Q. What are the duties of Christians towards princes who govern
  them? In particular what are our duties to Napoleon, our
  Emperor?
  A. Christians owe to the princes who govern them, and we, in
5 particular owe to Napoleon I, our Emperor, our love and respect,
  obedience loyalty and military service, and the taxes ordered for
  the defence of the Empire and his throne . . .
  Q. Why are we bound in these duties to our Emperor?
  A. . . . because God creates Empires and apportions them
10 according to his will, and has set him up as our sovereign and
  made him the agent of his power, and his image on earth. So to
  honour and serve the Emperor is to honour and serve God
  himself . . .

Napoleon also angered Pius VII by ordering, without reference to him, that the Church throughout the Empire should celebrate 16 August (the day after his own birthday) as St Napoléon's Day, unceremoniously removing from the calendar of saints the existing occupant of that date. The cult of the Emperor had reached its peak.

Such blatant interference in church affairs for political and personal advantage, made it obvious that Napoleon's religious activities were intended solely to produce loyal soldiers and civil servants. The fact that the Emperor was not interested in whether or not they were also good Catholics was brought home to the Pope by Napoleon's increasingly liberal attitude towards those Protestants and Jews prepared to be good and loyal French citizens. For example, Protestant ministers came to be treated in the same way as Catholic priests, as paid employees of the state. However, much worse things were in store for Pius VII (see page 66) in the days to come.

## 3 The Hundred Days – a Change of Heart?

When Napoleon returned to France in 1815 after his escape from exile in Elba, he appeared to many to have changed his political beliefs. His new policies were a complete *volteface* – an unexpected shock to many old supporters, a pleasant surprise to most old enemies. Even before he reached Paris he had announced that he proposed to govern France constitutionally 'according to the interests and will of the nation'. Was he sincere in his proposals for a constitutional monarchy based on complete freedom of expression, a two-chamber parliament with an elected lower chamber and a hereditary peerage?

An astonished Benjamin Constant, his long-time liberal opponent who had warned Sieyès against Napoleon in 1799, was invited to draw up the *Acte Additionel* (or the *Benjamine* as the new constitution was nicknamed). After a long conversation in which Napoleon appears to have convinced Constant that he was sincere in wishing to 'give the people liberty' by introducing free elections, ministerial freedom of action, free discussion and a free press, the invitation was accepted. Constant justified his decision in a rather convoluted explanation that the Emperor was carrying out these 'democratic measures' while still 'in possession of the dictatorship, and at a time when, had the Emperor wished for despotism, he could have tried to retain it. It may be said', Constant continued, 'that such an attempt would not be in his interest – doubtless that is true; but is not that as much as to say that his interest accords with public liberty? and is not that a reason for confidence in his sincerity?'

There were other views. A staunch Bonapartist wrote:

1 Whatever the personal prestige of the Emperor when defeated
  and dethroned he was not the same man when he returned to
  power. He posed as a liberal, compulsorily, against his will,
  self-mutilated . . . When even sincere Bonapartists cried 'We are
5 your men, but on conditions: there must be no more despotism,
  but liberty, a constitution, guarantees' . . . he was caught between

two fires – that of his own nature and habits and that of the necessities of the situation – he was unmanned. He was no longer himself.

Fouché, the former Minister of Police, who had deserted Napoleon in 1814, was even more condemnatory:

This man has been cured of nothing and returns as much a despot, as eager for conquests, in fact as mad as ever . . . The whole of Europe will fall on him . . .

The *Acte* was put to a plebiscite notable only for the massive abstention rate among the voters who had little enthusiasm for the 'new' Napoleon. Although he spoke publicly of the 1815 constitution as 'our rallying point, our pole star in hours of tempest', he seems privately to have regarded the *Acte* as simply a temporary concession to public opinion, a sop to the liberals without whose support he could not hope to rally the country to meet the coming Allied attack. Napoleon seems to have intended that the *Acte Additione* should be thought of not as a new constitution, but, as its name implied, an addition to the existing one. So he could, and did claim that the proposed two-tier parliament of 1815 was not the result of a freestanding *Acte*, but the direct and logical development of the Napoleonic legislative bodies and the Senate. This in its turn enabled his supporters to claim that a liberal empire resulted naturally from an authoritarian state when the time was ripe. However, there seems little doubt that in reality Napoleon would, as he admitted later, have taken the opportunity of his first military victory to dismiss the parliament and return France to a dictatorship.

## 4 The Nature of the Napoleonic Régime

What kind of régime was it that Napoleon had given France? The vast majority of historians would agree that Napoleon was a dictator – but was he a military dictator?

Napoleon had come to power by virtue of his reputation as a successful general and, at least until 1812, he retained the devotion of the ordinary soldier by virtue of his personal qualities of leadership, and his ability to win victories. From 1800 onwards there was what might be termed a certain 'militarisation' of society. With a general as head of state, and with universal conscription, it surprised no one that preference was shown to military personnel in awards of the Legion of Honour and of titles and estates, and that the *lycées* were organised along military lines. As the country was at war for most of Napoleon's time in power it was inevitable that the army should be very much in evidence, garrisoned in the towns or on the move along the roads – but at no time after the end of the *coup* was the army used by the government to interfere directly in politics, as had happened under the Directory. The role of the army at home was purely social. It took no part in implementing government policies and was not used by the authorities to control or intimidate the civilian population (apart from the suppression of unrest in the royalist west).

There was no large influx of military personnel into the administration either. Napoleon himself said:

1 France would never submit to a military government . . . Any attempt of that kind is bound to fail and ruin the man who makes it. It is not as a general I am governing France: it is because the nation believes that I possess the civil qualities (foresight, power 5 of calculation, administrative ability, ready wit, eloquence . . . and above all knowledge of men) which go to make a ruler.

Nor was Napoleon's France a police state, although it is sometimes described as such. It is true that apart from the Habsburg Empire in no other state to date had the police played such a prominent part in society or had such all embracing powers; but Napoleon's police bear little resemblance to the armed thugs of a modern police state. The general police might be sometimes arbitrary, sometimes brutal, but they did not, except on rare occasions, act outside the law. Only criminals needed to fear arrest – only lawbreakers were involved. Much more dangerous, because more insidious, was the government control of private conduct and opinion through a network of informers of all kinds. There were spies everywhere, some of them Fouché's, some Napoleon's. It was their presence which made life insecure for the many, and gave rise to the description of the régime as a police state.

Was Napoleon an 'Enlightened Despot'? Most historians would say no because, although he himself had been influenced in his youth by the Enlightenment, by its rationalism, its secularised society and its quasi-scientific principles, in later life he showed no sympathy for the political or moral ideas of the *philosophes* or *idéologues*. Many of them had supported the *coup d'état* of 1799, believing that Napoleon agreed with their liberal ideas on freedom and justice. They quickly discovered their error as they were manoeuvred out of political life, and, one of the most intelligent and influential of them, Madame de Staël, was forced into exile. There are, however, British historians who consider, as Markham does, that Napoleon 'in his mentality and his policy has much in common with the enlightened despots of the eighteenth century' and that in fact he has a 'strong claim to be the last and greatest' of them. What grounds are there for this argument?

A concentration on domestic reforms and peaceful policies rather than on foreign affairs and war was one of the hallmarks of government by an enlightened despot, and, in the early years of the Consulate this was true of Napoleon. According to the *philosophes* an enlightened

despot should favour moderate government, and should act rationally
to reform the state. He should rule by good laws which would bring his
people freedom and happiness. This could, however, only be done by
the exercise of absolute power, because there was no other way of
achieving practical results, but the ruler should have the welfare of his
people always at heart.

It was during the period of comparative peace from 1800 to 1803 that
Napoleon introduced the majority of his administrative, financial, legal,
religious and social changes, as well as the constitutional measures
which made the French head of state again an absolute ruler. In these
early years Napoleon did much that is reminiscent of many of the
enlightened despots of the previous century. He spoke publicly of the
need for moderate government. He reorganised the country's finances,
centralised the administration, curbed the power of the church

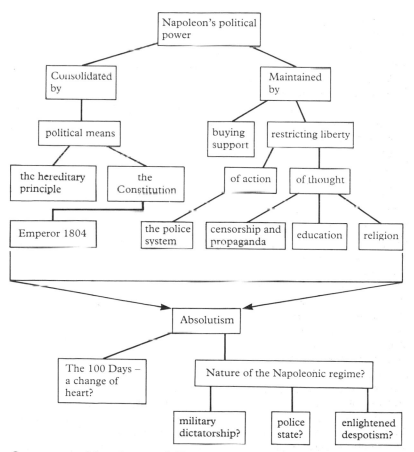

*Summary – Napoleon and France : Politics and Power*

(although he came to an understanding with the Pope in doing so), recodified the laws, reformed the judicial system and tinkered with education. He also built up the army – almost everywhere in the latter half of the eighteenth century the underlying motive of the enlightened ruler in embarking on his reforms was the establishment of his country as a military power. In 1803 war was resumed and was to occupy Napoleon to the exclusion of everything else for the remainder of his career; and enlightened despotism developed into dictatorship.

Some historians believe that from the first Napoleon had his sights set on dictatorship, perhaps even on the throne. Others would argue that this is doubtful, if only because he was an opportunist, not given to planning his actions any distance ahead but guided by changing circumstances.

In the first months after the *coup* the circumstances were not favourable to him. He knew that his hold on power was not strong. He was inexperienced in government. He had to move with circumspec-tion, not favouring one party against another, for he could easily be ousted in another *coup* if things went wrong. He had to win a convincing military victory quickly after Brumaire if he was to give stability to the new government and keep himself at the head of it. 'Conquest has made me what I am and conquest alone can maintain me'. The victory over the Austrians at Marengo in June 1800 (see page 128) and the peace treaties which followed, gave his personal prestige the boost it needed and made him and his government secure for the next 14 years.

---

*Making notes on 'Napoleon and France: Politics and Power'*

This is a chapter on which you need to make detailed notes. It contains a great deal of information on an important examination topic – how Napoleon maintained and extended the power he gained at Brumaire – and ends with a discussion on the nature of his régime.

Using the following headings should help you make your notes, and you may find afterwards writing a brief answer to each of the accompanying questions a useful way of summarising your informa-tion:

1  The Consolidation of Power
   a) The Constitution (How did Napoleon manipulate the situation to his advantage? – the electoral system; the plebiscites; dictatorship)
   b) The Hereditary Principle (How and why did Napoleon establish this? – Life Consulship; Emperor; the dynasty)
2  Maintaining Power
   a) By Buying Support (Whom did Napoleon bribe and with what?)

b)  By Restricting Liberty (What means did Napoleon use? – police, censorship, propaganda, education, religion)

3  The Hundred Days (Did Napoleon have a change of heart?)

4  The nature of the régime (How do you consider Napoleon's régime is best described? Why?)

---

*Answering Essay questions on 'Napoleon and France: Politics and Power'*

Many examination questions on Napoleon's power in France are of the 'How, why, what' type. For example:

1  How did Napoleon consolidate his power in France?

2  Why was there so little opposition to Napoleon's régime in France?

3  What means did Napoleon use to establish himself as absolute ruler of France between 1800 and 1804?

4  What were Napoleon's most important domestic achievements during the Consulate?

5  How did Napoleon ensure support for his domestic policies?

All these questions are straightforward requests for factual information. They are best dealt with by first making a list of points which you want to include in your answer, and then deciding in which order it would be most effective to present them. Would you, for instance, start with the most or with the least important? What criteria would you choose in deciding the order? When dates are included (as in question 3) be careful both to stay within the time-span and to cover the whole of it.

Question 2 is a typical 'why?' question and is most easily answered by making a plan based on a list of points all starting 'because'. In this case you could include:

a)  because of his efficient spy system

b)  because of his censorship of news

c)  because of his propaganda machine.

You need a list of five or six points, each of which can be expanded into a full paragraph containing detailed information to support your 'paragraph point'. Do not forget an introduction and conclusion will also be needed. What is their purpose, and how would you hope to achieve it?

The next chapter also deals with 'Napoleon and France' and you may prefer to wait until you have studied that before you answer any of the above essay questions.

*Source-based questions on 'Napoleon and France: Politics and Power'*

## 1 The Constitution

Carefully read the extracts on pages 74, 75 and 76, and answer the following questions:

a) What is the tone of the first extract (page 74)? How does it differ from those on page 76? Illustrate your answer with specific examples. *(7 marks)*

b) What does the second extract (page 74) give as the reasons for the *coup*? Are they justified? Explain your answer. *(5 marks)*

c) Comment on the last sentence (lines 12–14) of the extract. How does the wording differ from lines 4–5 of the extract on page 76? *(4 marks)*

d) What on page 75 are the grounds for Constant's anxiety? Was he justified in his concern? *(4 marks)*

## 2 The Coronation

Carefully read the extracts on page 80 and 81. Answer the following questions.

a) In the extract on page 80 explain 'the great people' (line 3). What reason does Napoleon give for returning to a hereditary monarchy? How far was the reason a valid one? *(4 marks)*

b) In the extract on page 81 explain 'Concordat' (line 2). What was meant by 'the irrevocability of the sale of national property' (line 3) and what was important about it? *(5 marks)*

c) In what respects does the coronation oath differ from the oath taken by Napoleon after Brumaire? (page 74, lines 12–14). Was the difference significant? Explain your answer? *(6 marks)*

## 3 The Spy Network

Carefully read the extracts on pages 85 and 86 and answer the following questions:

a) What is the difference between the spies of the first extract and those of the second? Who were their respective employers? *(4 marks)*

b) What do these two extracts suggest about the efficiency of the spy system and about relations between Napoleon and the people? Support your answer with quotations from the extracts. *(6 marks)*

## 4 Education and Religion

Carefully read the extracts on pages 89, 90 and 91 and answer the following questions:

a) Comment on Napoleon's views on the role of education, given on page 89. How can they best be described in their totality? *(3 marks)*

b) What is the fallacy in Napoleon's argument on page 90 in favour of a social need for religion? *(2 marks)*

c) In the extract on page 91 what relationship between Church and State is envisaged by Napoleon? Illustrate your answer with specific examples. *(5 marks)*

# CHAPTER 7

# Napoleon and France: 'Son of the Revolution'?

## 1 Napoleon and the Revolution

How can 'Napoleon and the Revolution' be best described? Was he its heir, carrying on its policies and maintaining its ideals, or did he betray it and bring it to an end with a return to the policies of the Ancien Régime? Or was he, as he often declared, a bridge between the old and the new, combining the best of both worlds?

Napoleon's relationship with the Revolution was a changing one. It altered with the passage of time and according to circumstances. On a number of occasions in the early part of his career he claimed to be a 'son of the Revolution', the staunch upholder of its principles, and the inheritor of its teachings on liberty, and equality. The proclamation of 15 December 1799 outlining the new Constitution announced firmly that 'the Revolution has been stablised on the principles which began it'. Two years later, with rather less revolutionary zeal, he told the Council of State, 'We have finished the romance of the Revolution, we must now begin its history, only seeking for what is real and practicable in the application of its principles'. After becoming Emperor he frequently promised that 'the French Revolution need fear nothing, since the throne of the Bourbons is occupied by a soldier' and at the end of 1812 he was still talking of his 'firm resolve to make the most of all that the Revolution had produced which was great and good'. However, his support for revolutions in general had waned: 'Since I have worn a crown I have shown clearly that I mean to close the doors against revolution. The sovereigns of Europe are indebted to me for stemming the revolutionary torrent which threatened their thrones'. He began to see himself as a personal peacemaker between revolutionaries and royalists: 'The greatest seigneurs of the old régime now dine with former revolutionaries. My government has brought about this fusion'. In the same year, 1812, he addressed the Council of State on certain 'errors' made by the *idéologues* of the Revolution, 'to which every misfortune experienced by our beautiful France must be attributed'. He asked the Council:

1 Who proclaimed the principle that rebellion was a duty? Who fawned on the people by proclaiming its sovereignty, which it was incapable of exercising? Who destroyed the awe and sanctity of the laws by making them depend, not on the sacred principles of
5 justice, not on the natural order, not on civil law, but merely on the will of an assembly whose members were ignorant of civil, penal, administrative, political and military laws?

He who has been called upon to regenerate a state must follow absolutely opposite principles.

Once he reached St Helena the Legend took over (see page 130) and the talk there in 1816 and until his death was of Napoleon as the great protagonist of the Revolution and guardian of its achievements, the 'prince of liberal opinions':

1 Let me charge you to respect liberty; and above all equality. With regard to liberty, it might be possible to restrain it in a case of extremity . . . but heaven forbid that we should ever infringe upon equality! It is the passion of the age; and I wish to continue
5 to be the man of the age!
The great battle of the century had been won and the Revolution accomplished; now all that remained was to reconcile it with all that it had not destroyed. That task belonged to me. I became the arch of the alliance between the old and the new, the natural
10 mediator between the old and the new orders. I maintained the principles and possessed the confidence of the one; I had identified myself with the other. I belonged to them both.

In a highflown vein he continued:

I closed the gulf of anarchy and cleared away the chaos. I purified the Revolution, dignified nations and established kings. I excited every kind of emulation, rewarded every kind of merit, and extended the limits of glory.

* Napoleon was already an army officer, aged 20, when the Revolution began in 1789. He was immediately caught up in the excitement and became an ardent patriot, although his enthusiasm was temporarily dampened in September 1792 after witnessing the storming of the Tuileries, and the massacre which followed (his life-long fear of crowds is generally thought to date from this time). Much later he expressed the view that a revolution however justified 'is one of the greatest evils by which mankind can be visited' because of the violence and suffering it brings in its train, but was able to console himself by reaffirming his belief that 'The Emperor [by his policies] has healed the wounds which the Revolution inflicted'.
The importance to Napoleon of the property-owning classes, both established landowners and those who had benefited from the purchase of *biens nationaux* during the Revolution, was discussed in the previous chapter (page 79). It is not surprising that property figures prominently among the revolutionary principles on which the Constitution of 1799 was alleged to be founded. These were listed not, as in 1789, as liberty,

equality, fraternity, but as representative government, the sacred rights of property, equality and liberty. It is worth noting that the 1799 Constitution avoids any explicit reference to the Rights of Man and of the Citizen (1789) and that fraternity has disappeared from it altogether, while equality and liberty (in that order) are preceded by property. Napoleon asserted over and over again that the preservation of liberty and equality were at all times his chief concern, but his actions too often belied his words for his excuses about extreme pressure of circumstances to carry much weight with his critics. He insisted as well that he maintained the principles and preserved the positive gains of the Revolution; but how far do his domestic policies actually accord with his declared Revolutionary ideals? Do not some at least have a flavour of the Ancien Régime?

## 2 Revolutionary Ideals in Practice?

Napoleon may have put 'representative government' as the first revolutionary principle of his 1799 Constitution, but he was at pains to ensure by means of his new 'electoral' systems (see page 76 and the diagram on page 77) that it would not be effectively implemented, nor would executive power be divided.

### a) Government and Administration

Modern research has shown that in some ways Brumaire was not a watershed, separating the Consulate from the Directory as completely as was once thought. A great deal of detailed investigation has been made into the composition of the legislative bodies, the central bureaucracy and the provincial administration during the Consulate. In all cases there is a clear continuity of personnel from pre-Brumairean days – of the first 300 members of the Legislature, for instance, 240 had been members of the Directory councils, as had been 69 of the 100 first members of the Tribunate. Most of the first holders of senior administrative posts had been in office at the time of the *coup*. They were just taken over by the new régime, and this link with the past helped to stabilise Napoleon's government in its early days. In provincial administration, 76 of the first prefects appointed had been members of various Revolutionary assemblies. Most of them were in their mid-forties, many with considerable experience as ministers or high-ranking executives during the previous decade.

The Council of State chosen, appointed and presided over by Napoleon, had at the end of 1799 a membership of 29, all of whom were men of high ability and half of whom were well experienced in government service under the Directory. The Council, which was a consultative not an executive body, was used by Napoleon, especially during the Consulate, to bypass the Legislature by issuing Orders in

Council. The various ministries were subordinated to it, and therefore to Napoleon himself, and their activities were co-ordinated through the Secretariat (later the Ministry) of State, an institution itself taken over from the Directory.

* If there was a continuity of staff from the Directory, there were, on the other hand, organisational similarities to the Ancien Régime to be found in Napoleon's government structure.

The Council of State itself was a revival under a more acceptable name of the old Royal Council, by which the the Kings of France had governed. The provincial administration imposed by Napoleon also bore a marked resemblance to that of the Bourbons. It was once again, as in pre-Revolutionary days, a centralised organisation. Government appointed officials (prefects, sub-prefects and mayors) replaced the devolved, loosely controlled and locally elected but inefficient system of local government favoured by the Directory. Although Napoleon retained the *départements* of the Revolution, he reintroduced the 40,000 pre-1789 communes as his basic territorial and 'electoral' unit. (The communes had had a chequered career during the Revolution, being suppressed in 1791, then revived by the Jacobins, and finally abolished in 1795). The prefect's role was an important one, the link between the people and the ruler. It is often likened to that of 'the *intendant* writ large' (the *intendants* were the local royal officials of the Ancien Régime) because the latter's powers had been limited by the authority of the *parlements* and Provincial Estates. No such curbs existed for the prefect, for the local councils, nominated, like the officials, by the government, had no real independence. The provincial judicature became similarly centralised when appointed judges replaced the elected ones of the Revolution and new Courts of Appeal were established. The system for collecting direct taxes was also reorganised centrally and local tax-collectors appointed for the purpose.

* Once the Consulate became hereditary it became to all intents and purposes a monarchy. Napoleon, despite his revolutionary past, openly admired certain aspects of the Bourbon régime, and described 'the old administration . . . [as] the most perfect that ever existed'. He saw the Revolution as entirely compatible with monarchy and believed that if Louis XVI had been more adaptable he could have remained king. As it was, his death left the way open for Napoleon to 'pick a crown out of the gutter' and establish the 'fourth dynasty of France'. In 1804 Napoleon became 'by the grace of God and the Constitution, Emperor of the French' – he seems to have decided against adopting the title 'King of France' in deference to revolutionary sensibilities, and to avoid a direct comparision with the monarchical past. In any case his ambitions had outgrown the idea of a mere kingdom; he already saw himself at the head of a 'universal empire' (see page 65).

This all seems a far cry from the doctrines of 1789, but some historians argue otherwise. They believe that by retaining the words

*République Francaise* on official documents until 1804 and on the reverse of his coins until 1809 Napoleon was demonstrating to the people that his government, both Consulate and Empire, was a continuation of the Revolution. On the other hand, there are historians who consider that when, after his consecration by the Pope, Napoleon took the crown from the altar, raised it above the congregation and placed it on his own head, he was showing that sovereignty no longer belonged to the people as in Republican days but had been transferred absolutely to him and his heirs for ever. Yet other historians see the coronation ceremony variously as brought about by family pressure on Napoleon to found a hereditary dynasty, with all the advantages that could be expected to bring to his brothers and sisters in the way of titles and lands, or, less convincingly, as a conciliatory gesture to the royalists and a means of encouraging their acceptance of the new emperor in place of the old king; or, rather more probably, as a bid for equality and respectability among the crowned heads of Europe. The presence of the Pope at Notre Dame certainly gave Napoleon a prestige he could not otherwise have acquired, while making it plain to the rest of the world that the Church had given its blessing to an Empire sprung from a Revolution it had previously denounced. Indeed, on the eve of the Austrian marriage in 1810 (which itself was seen by many Frenchmen as a betrayal of the Revolution) Napoleon, entertaining what he called a 'garden of kings', presented himself to them as a fellow monarch welcoming his royal neighbours.

The lack of any popular representation in either of his régimes would not have worried Napoleon, for his view of sovereignty of the people had become far removed from that of Rousseau's *Social Contract*, a classic statement on the principles of republican government, which had much influenced Napoleon's political ideas as a young man. By 1804 Napoleon considered that sovereignty of the people in no way implied the right of the people to a say in government, but simply gave them the right to have a ruler who governed them as the majority of them wished to be governed – and that he had fulfilled his obligations by giving them the strong, autocratic government he believed most of them wanted.

There are historians who consider that the Empire was in effect a 'dictatorship of public safety' in the revolutionary mode, its introduction brought about by the 'illogical expectation' that by imposing hereditary rule any further danger from intrigues, plots and assassination attempts which were undermining the stability of the government, would be overcome. It has been argued by one Marxist historian that Napoleon, by imposing an oath of loyalty on all government officials, from the Emperor himself downwards, was strengthening the régime's 'public safety' aspect, and establishing a clear difference between his régime and that of the old despotic monarchies. However, such difference is not readily apparant in the decree of 1808 which established the imperial nobility, and in which Napoleon refers to the people not as citizens, but as his 'subjects'.

## b) Equality?

The abolition by the Revolution of feudal and other dues and services was confirmed by Napoleon, and equality before the law was more or less preserved in his Civil Code. The rights to the ownership of property in general, and to the continued enjoyment of *biens nationaux* acquired during the Revolution in particular, were also safeguarded. It was the award of honours, and of titles, which marked a break by Napoleon with the Revolution in the eyes of many of his contemporaries. What could be be more prejudicial to the idea of equality? What could be a more retrograde step than the creation of an élite? Napoleon tried, rather unconvincingly, to justify his actions. He pointed out that the titles carried no legal privileges or tax immunity, and that by establishing a nobility based on service to the state, not on birth, he had destroyed the old aristocracy. However, his argument was somewhat undermined by the fact that the newly ennobled could buy an entail and make their titles hereditary. In answer to criticisms of the Legion of Honour he spoke, equally unconvincingly, of it as a 'unique decoration', and of 'the universality of its application as the symbol of equality', and explained how 'I instituted the new nobility . . . to satisfy the people, as the greatest part of those I ennobled sprang from them – every private soldier had a right to expect he could earn the title of duke'.

* Is the old textbook cliché correct in claiming that Napoleon reconciled the aristocracy of the Ancien Régime with the bourgeoisie of the Revolution to form a new governing élite, which even men of humble origins could also aspire to join – the so-called 'politics of amalgamation'? French historians have studied the social make-up of the imperial nobility and have found that out of nearly 3500 men ennobled in the decade after 1804 just over 20 per cent came from the old nobility, nearly 60 per cent from the bourgeoisie and nearly 20 per cent from the people, with almost all of the latter owing their titles to military service (see page 83). Studies of the composition of lists of members of the Tribunate and Legislature have given rather similar results and seem to bear out the textbook statements. However, historians working on the membership of the *arondissement* and departmental electoral colleges have painted a different picture, with a far smaller percentage of old nobility and a much higher proportion of businessmen among the members. Other research on the lists of notables (the wealthy) drawn up by the prefects in each department has found that in this setting there are comparatively few men of humble origin, the great majority being members of the bourgeoisie, and the remainder former nobles, although few of these actually accepted office

under Napoleon. Despite all the research, the precise composition of Napoleon's governing élite is still uncertain, but what is clear is that the bourgeoisie were the dominant element.

\* One of Napoleon's favourite remarks was that he followed faithfully the Revolutionary precept that talent and courage should be rewarded without distinction of birth, 'provided they have the knowledge, the ability and the qualities'. This was a considerable exaggeration. As the new nobility could buy hereditary rights, so could money buy privilege and position. Without money, or at least influence and the right connections, there was little chance of much advancement in any sphere. A number of French historians have examined statistical information on career opportunities. The opportunities for improving their social and economic status seem to have been extremely limited for agricultural workers. A few managed to acquire a small plot of land, although seldom enough to support a family, especially as the land which became available after 1800 was usually of very poor quality. It was apparantly a good deal easier for artisans to move into the urban lower middle class and set up a small business, although they were unlikely to be able to develop it very far because the business world was largely in the hands of only a few, well-established families, many of whom had risen to prominence through the world of banking.

In the professions, too, the way to the top was barred. There were large numbers of poorly paid posts in the bureaucracy, for instance, but without good educational qualifications there was no hope of promotion and to get such qualifications was not easy for those of humble origin. Sons of officers could be educated free in the *lycées*, but others had to pay, there and in the secondary schools. Church-run private schools were expensive, primary schools were almost non-existent and the people as a whole were illiterate. There were clearly strict educational limits to the 'career open to talents'. Clerks in the bureaucracy did not become heads of department, nor heads of department become ministers. Even in cases where the young man of good family had completed a course in the *lycée* he might find that this was not enough. The Audit Office, established in 1803 as a training ground for young recruits aspiring to the highest government posts, required candidates for appointment to it to have an income of 6000 francs a year. This 'officially removed from the rank of auditor all less well-off young men, however well educated, however gifted, hardworking and well bred they may be' as one aspirant to office complained. One who did manage to become an auditor commented that the principal obstacle to doing so was finding the necessary fortune. Napoleon's government was increasingly staffed by a money-based bureacracy. In the bureaucracy, if not elsewhere, there were further bars to promotion however able the candidate. Too often in practice it was promotion by seniority not merit and, given Napoleon's preference for obedient servants rather than independent thinkers, the best did not always reach the top.

In the army promotion from the conscripted levies for a peasant lad was difficult, and the chances of reaching any rank higher than that of lieutenant extremely unlikely. The exceptions, men like Ney and Murat who rose to be marshals, can be counted on the fingers of one hand. A fair number of Napoleon's generals were from military families and of noble origin, but most came from the bourgeoisie. Despite the saying attributed to Napoleon that every soldier carried a fieldmarshal's baton in his knapsack, no private soldier ever found one there.

Even in the matter of conscription there was inequality of opportunity to avoid it. The proportion of young men liable for call up varied from region to region, an arrangement which was clearly unfair. The reasons for the variations were usually political or military – the Vendée, for instance, with its strongly royalist tradition was favourably treated in the hope of mollifying its inhabitants, while frontier departments in the east and open to foreign attack were up to five times more heavily assessed. In addition, under a law passed in 1800, a rich man could avoid conscription by paying a substitute to serve in his place, and something between 5 and 10 per cent of those conscripted did so. As time went by and losses in battle rose, so too did the price of substitutes. By 1811 even the poorest peasant needed a substantial inducement to join the army, and the price reached a figure of about nine times the annual income of an unskilled labourer.

Taxation was another area of inequality. The Directory had revived the pre-revolutionary practice of levying indirect taxes, but it was the Empire which expanded them to provide the major part of the revenue needed to pay for the war. On the grounds of good financial practice, the burden of taxation was increasingly shifted from direct to indirect taxation – that is from the well-to-do property-owners, to the consumers, the majority of whom were poor. Taxes on land rose only slowly, while the yield of indirect taxes increased by 50 per cent in the decade to 1814. In 1802 taxes on tobacco, playing cards, alcohol and some other goods were regrouped into the unpopular *droits réunis*. In 1806 a tax on salt, unpleasantly reminiscent of the *gabelle* of the Ancien Régime, was introduced, and four years later the old state monopoly on tobacco was re-established

## c) Liberty?

During the Hundred Days Napoleon, in the course of a long conversation with Benjamin Constant (see page 92), defended his past illiberal actions on the grounds of political necessity. 'I am not an enemy of liberty', he said, '[but] I set it aside when it obstructed my way'. And set it aside he did, restricting liberty of action and freedom of expression, moulding thought and belief, and imposing absolute political authority. His law codes, particularly the Criminal and Penal Codes, were much closer to the practices of the Ancien Régime than to those of the Revolution. The use of censorship and propaganda, the practice of indoctrination through the militarised *lycées* and via the Imperial Catechism, the activities of the spy network and of the police, all played a part in the establishment and maintenance of the Napoleonic state – at the expense of liberty.

In 1814 when Napoleon was facing the Allied invasion of France – the first time foreign troops had been on French soil since 1793 – his advisers begged him to call on the memories of those Revolutionary days and rally the people to the country's defence. 'How can I', said Napoleon, 'when I myself have destroyed the Revolution?'.

## 3 Assessment

Napoleon's own preference was always for authoritarian rule – 'I do not believe that the French love liberty and equality', he told the Council of State in 1802. 'Ten years of revolution has not changed them'. He himself had little time for representative bodies, but he seems to have felt a sense of guilt about his failure to govern with the aid of a parliament of the kind which he admired in England. He excused his failure to do so by blaming the politicians, whom he considered to be irresponsible self-seekers likely to undermine the stability of the state if they were given the opportunity to air their political opinions in public. Successive Revolutionary governments had made all posts open to direct election. Popular participation, though, had been disappointing, with voting levels low, and there was little public protest when Napoleon abolished elections for all administrative and judicial posts. Officials of all kinds (even JPs from 1806) were subsequently appointed instead, most of them chosen by Napoleon himself from names on the electoral college lists. Napoleon's France was an autocracy operated through a centralised and efficient bureaucracy.

Napoleon's domestic policy in many areas was not only a move away from the ideals of the Revolution and a reversion to at least some of the practices of the Ancien Régime, it was also a foretaste of the dictatorships of the twentieth century. Napoleonic France may not have been a military dictatorship but it was certainly a militaristic state, geared to war and conquest. To Napoleon *La Gloire* was as important as it had been to Louis XIV a century earlier and territorial aggrandisment as important as it was to be to Hitler a century later. For all three rulers the achievement of these ambitions was dependent upon their absolute authority at home. Napoleon expressed this openly when he spoke of his desire for 'the empire of the world' and how, in order to ensure it, 'unlimited power was necessary to me' (see chapters 3 and 4 ).

'Napoleon: reformer, revolutionary or reactionary?' is an old question to which there is no clear answer. The centralisation of government, for instance, can be seen either as a reform of the loose control exercised by the Directory, or as the first steps to absolutism and a return to pre-Revolutionary days, while the Civil Code can be judged to be either a completion of the unifying work begun during the Revolution or a reactionary set of Articles restoring the paternal authority of Roman Law. Perhaps it is more realistic to say that Napoleon, as an opportunist, rang the changes on reformer, revolutionary or reactionary as best suited him at the time. Not surprisingly, therefore, a number of his institutions represent a pragmatic compromise between the Revolution and the Ancien Régime – the Concordat, for example, officially abandoned the Revolutionary anti-clerical line, while at the same time obtaining official Papal recognition that the sale of church lands was irrevocable.

## 4 Napoleon's Effects on France

How much did France change in the years 1799 to 1815 under Napoleon's rule, what effects did he have on the country, and how long did they last? It used to be generally accepted that remarkable and far-reaching changes were made in France by Napoleon. Now historians are less certain about this, and there are a number who argue that there was a much greater continuity with the Revolution and/or with the Ancien Régime (see page 102) than was previously believed, that France changed less in the Napoleonic period than during the shorter Revolutionary one, and that comparatively little of Napoleon's work outlived his régime. What is the evidence?

Of course there *were* changes – political, constitutional, legal and religious – under Napoleon, which affected, by his direct intent, the way individuals thought and the way they lived; and there were other of his activities, his obsession with war for instance, which affected society more indirectly. Some effects outlasted the Napoleonic era, and some did not.

In the first category of direct action, are his governmental and administrative reforms which replaced the popular sovereignty of the Revolution (loosely controlled, devolved government based on a system of elections) with a centralised autocratic rule not unlike that of the Ancien Régime, especially after the establishment of the Empire in 1804. So too, his legal and judicial reforms based on the authoritarianism of Roman law, his suppression of freedom of expression and his extension of police powers smacked more of the Bourbon monarchy than of the Revolution (see pages 84–88). In present-day terminology, Napoleon's human rights record was not good. Behaviour was regimented and beliefs were moulded through education, propaganda and censorship, spies were everywhere, and opposition was vigorously rooted out. All life was geared to the service of the state and its ruler in a way never previously seen in France, even in the time of Louis XIV.

It would be easy, though, to exaggerate the repressive nature of Napoleon's rule and to forget that (even allowing for the fact that it would have been almost impossible in practice for him to have put them into reverse) he *did* maintain the great gains of the Revolution by confirming in the Constitution and the Civil Code the end of feudalism in France and the equality of Frenchmen before the law, and in the Concordat the irrevocability of the sale of the *biens nationaux*.

What were the more general effects of Napoleon on France?

## a) On Society

Our knowledge of social conditions, especially among the poor, in Napoleonic France is patchy and inconclusive. Comparatively little research has been done on the less wealthy elements of society in either town or country.

From those local studies which have been carried out it seems that agricultural wages rose only slowly in the years 1800–15 and hardly kept pace with prices and rents. The latter rose sharply due to the increased demand for land. The reasons for this increased demand are uncertain. Some historians attribute it to a sharp growth in population, but this idea is disputed by others (see below, page 111). Where land *did* become available for purchase only, holdings of poor quality and under five hectares in area were within the peasants' financial grasp. All the better land was bought up by members of the bourgeoisie, but having acquired it, they did little with it, regarding its possession simply as a status symbol and a sound investment. There was no agricultural revolution at this time and farming continued in the old unimproved subsistence tradition. This may have been partly because until 1811, the harvests were particularly good. Food was therefore plentiful and cheap and the people were reasonably content. There seemed no need to worry about improving stockbreeding or increasing crop production. It was part of Napoleon's 'luck' that France enjoyed a decade of good harvests and with them peace in the countryside. It was not until the bad harvest of 1811, followed by the extra conscription burdens of 1812–14, that he was faced with any serious social unrest.

Current historical opinion is that despite the good harvests and the end of feudalism there seems to have been at least as much rural poverty in the later years of the Empire as there had been before 1789; but the situation was patchy, and in some regions, particularly the cereal-growing areas of the north, contemporaries report an overall improvement in peasant dress, housing and diet.

Napoleon was politically so committed to the beneficiaries of the Revolution that his social policies were of the most conservative kind in relation to the rural and urban poor. He liked to speak of how the French people loved him as the 'People's King' or as the peasants' friend, but it is difficult to see why either he or they should have believed it. He did nothing for the mass of the people except take their sons for the army and tax them for its support. The continual levying of young men and the markedly more efficient arrangements for the collection of taxes directly affected the peasants much more than any other class of society. Yet they were the ones who cheered his return from Elba in 1815. He ascribed their support to the rapport which he said had always existed between him and his peasants, but it seems more likely that it was for them at that time a question of 'the devil you know' – fear that feudalism would return along with the Bourbons was very real to the mass of the people. After 1815 the mythical figure of the 'Emperor of the common man' was created in the popular mind largely as a reaction to Bourbon favouritism towards the aristocracy.

So few statistics are available about the urban working class that it is unclear whether there was a shortage of labour in the towns caused by the war, or whether, on the contrary, there was an excess of labour brought about by an influx of peasants from the countryside and of deserters from the army. Either way, conditions for workers were bad, particularly after the ban on workers' coalitions was reaffirmed in 1803 and, although there is little information on exactly how much the *livret* (see page 85) was used, it must always have threatened a worker's right to seek new employment. Napoleon seems to have regarded the urban workers with the gravest suspicion, believing them to be troublemakers who needed firm handling and close police supervision.

Even the more prosperous elements of society are not well understood. Although a good deal of research has been done, most of it has been concerned with investigations into the make-up of the Napoleonic élite (see page 102) culled from the interminable lists prepared by prefects and others, most of which furnish no more than name, wealth and occupation and tell us nothing about the people and their families and how they lived.

* What effect did Napoleon's long wars have on the population of France? The slow growth rate of the French population, in comparison with that of other western European countries, during the nineteenth century used to be attributed to the heavy loss of life among young men drafted into his army. Recent demographic research suggests, however, that this explanation is inadequate because the fall in the birth-rate had begun even before the Revolution.

For reasons not entirely understood, young people began to marry earlier from the late 1780s onwards, but at the same time to have smaller families. The earlier marriage can be explained after 1792 by the young men's anxiety to avoid conscription, but the fall by some 20 per cent in the birth rate in the last quarter of the eighteenth century is more difficult to understand. It is suggested that after 1789, with the reduction of traditional moral pressures from the church and society, birth control came to be widely practised, and that the series of economic catastrophes during the 1790s together with the Revolutionary laws on property inheritance (*partage*) (see page 85) may also have helped to keep families small.

*Did* Napoleon's wars have an effect on population growth? The answer would appear to be, yes, but to a much lesser extent than the old textbooks suggested. Of the two million men who found themselves in the army between 1800 and 1814 the number killed, who died of wounds, disease, hunger or cold, or who simply went missing believed killed, has been estimated at 916,000. This figure is usually quoted as representing about 7 per cent of the total population of France; but that is misleading because the losses were not spread evenly across the population. They fell heavily on the young men of marriageable age – a devastating 38 per cent of men born in the years 1790–95 were killed, the majority of them between 1812 and 1814. To the extent that this must have left many young women without husbands, and have reduced further the already declining birth rate, Napoleon's wars must accept some of the blame, but only some, for the slow growth of the population in nineteenth-century France.

## b) On the Economy

Here again historians are in conflict. Did France develop industrially under Napoleon or was the economy in a state of stagnation? Did the Continental Blockade benefit France or was it a disaster?

### i) Industry
In 1785 the economic development of Britain and France was comparable. But in the next 15 years, while Britain was forging ahead in industrial development, the upheavals of the Revolution held France back. Some historians have suggested that by 1800 France too was on the edge of an industrial revolution. Their argument is chiefly based on advances in the cotton industry. French imports of raw cotton more than doubled between 1803 and 1807, and a shortage of supplies from French colonies was made up until 1811 by overland shipments from the Levant which entered France through Strasbourg. In Paris alone the number of cotton-spinning firms grew from five to 57 in eight years, and in 1807 over 12,000 workers were employed in the industry there. This dramatic growth was due to mechanisation of spinning by the introduction of imitation British 'mule-jennies', and by the protectionist effect of the Continental Blockade on home production which removed the competition from British cotton cloth. But, despite its expansion, cotton did not become a factory-based industry – it remained a cottage one. Even in the largest spinning firm 90 per cent of its 8000 employees were scattered round Paris as home outworkers, and the same was true on the weaving side of the industry. There was no similar advance in any of the other textile industries. The great increase in cotton production was to their disadvantage. Linen and hemp

manufacturers found themselves facing declining demand and the silk and woollen industries suffered also from the fashionable preference for cotton dress materials during the Empire.

Other industries, too, developed only slowly in the Napoleonic period. The chemical industry did make some progress, developing artificial dyes and new bleaching materials for the cotton spinners and weavers, and experimenting with the production of artificial soda for the soap manufacturers of Marseilles. The iron industry benefited from the demand for armaments needed for Napoleon's wars, but failed to modernise itself, preferring the old method of smelting the ore with charcoal rather than coal.

On the information at present available, there is no evidence that in the early 1800s France was on the verge of an industrial revolution of the kind experienced in Britain. While Napoleon is said to have been keenly interested in French industry and to have provided manufacturers with substantial subsidies, it does not appear to have been one of his priorities. By 1815 little industrial progress had been made and the development of a factory system lay in the future.

The economy of the countryside was equally stagnant. Despite official encouragement land clearing and drainage made little headway. Yields did not increase and labour methods remained primitive. Landowners did not reinvest their rents in the land and no new techniques were developed. Any agricultural expansion which took place was simply an extension of the cultivated area. The only other development of any significance was a government programme for the growing of sugar-beet and chicory to fill gaps left by the colonially produced sugar and coffee no longer available under the rigours of the Continental Blockade.

## ii) The Continental Blockade 1806–13

The Continental Blockade was a two-pronged enterprise, a combined 'war-machine' and a 'market-design', intended to double as an economic weapon against Britain, and as a commercial shield for France.

In November 1806 Napoleon announced by the Berlin Decrees that the British Isles was officially in a state of blockade by land and sea and forbade any communication with them by France or any of her satellites. This was in response to a British naval blockade of the French coast, which had begun a few months earlier in May 1806. Early in 1807 the British extended their blockade. Neutral ships were required to call at British ports for inspection, to pay duties and to obtain licences before trading with French controlled ports. At the end of 1807 Napoleon countered with the Milan Decrees. These extended the embargo on British goods to all neutral ships which complied with the new British demands.

The Blockade as a 'war-machine' was intended to 'conquer Britain by excess'. British exports and re-exports were to be prevented from leaving the country and the unsold goods would then build up to such an extent that British trade would be brought to a standstill and her economy disrupted. If, at the same time *imports* into Britain were allowed, or even encouraged – on condition of cash payment in gold – this would help to drain away her bullion reserves and weaken her economy further. She would become unable to fulfil her main rôle in the Coalition against France – that of providing the ready money needed to maintain and equip the allied armies – and might well decide to settle for a separate peace before her position as a trading nation had been totally undermined.

The Blockade as a 'market-design' was intended to protect French home industries from British competition and to provide them with new European markets in the satellite and annexed states. In return these states would provide goods needed by France for home consumption or manufacture and re-export to the rest of the Empire. In this way Napoleon's European territories would form a self-sufficient commercial and trading enterprise, independent of foreign goods.

How well did these arrangements work for Napoleon? The operation of the 'war-machine' suffered from the beginning from the French lack of sea power. The situation worsened after most of the navy was destroyed at Trafalgar in 1805, and with an ineffective navy and with an incompetent and corrupt customs service, smuggling became endemic. Prohibited goods were brought in by British smugglers who dodged the Blockade with the help of French subjects all along the Atlantic and North Sea coasts. At least one historian has judged this to have been the most widespread form of civil disobedience to Napoleon's rule. In 1809 in an attempt to regularise the situation, increase customs revenues and get rid of a surplus of wine and grain stocks, Napoleon took drastic action against smugglers. He seized and destroyed contraband goods, and instituted a system of licences enabling French subjects to trade with the enemy. These new measures, by reducing opportunities for illicit trading with the continent, had a serious effect on the British economy. By 1811 Britain, in difficulties from the failed harvest of 1810 and the need to pay in gold for shipments of grain exported under licence from France, and with her own overseas trade lower than at any time since 1802, faced a potentially disastrous crisis in her balance of payments. The Blockade had been more successful as an economic weapon against Britain than is usually accepted. Without the catastrophe of the French invasion of Russia, (itself a byproduct of the Blockade), Britain's prospects would have been bleak; but by 1813 Napoleon, desperately in need of money to finance a new campaign, was issuing licences in such profusion that the Blockade was no longer of any significance as an economic weapon of war.

What were the effects of the Blockade on France? British historians have tended to concentrate on the maritime aspects, and this has led to a rather unbalanced view of what is a much more complex situation.

French historians have looked more at the general economic effects and it now seems that the effect of the Blockade on France was a mixed one.

There is no doubt that the ports of the Atlantic and Channel coasts did suffer quite severely from the loss of sea-borne trade, and from the British navy's counter-blockading activities. Shipbuilding and its associated maritime trades, such as rope-making and sail-making, declined and so too did inland industries which depended on overseas markets. The old established linen industries of the north and west of France, for instance, already in decline and technologically backward, were badly affected by the loss of exports. With the decline in opportunities for overseas trade and the consequent loss of profits, many of the older industries suffered from lack of capital. This underfunding was made more acute when many investors moved their money out of commercial enterprises into what now seemed to be the better security of land ownership. In consequence, several of the old merchant families and banking houses collapsed due to a general lack of business confidence.

All was not doom and gloom, however, for in some areas well away from the coasts, French subjects positively benefited for a time from the protection to home industries which the Blockade offered, and by the opportunity it provided to export goods across the Alps and the Rhine to outlying parts of the Empire. There the inhabitants, unable to buy legitimately elsewhere, had no choice but to pay the high prices demanded by French producers. As the British navy increasingly barred the sea-lanes to French goods, trade routes moved overland, away from the coast. Paris became an important trading centre for luxuries, and items of fashion, as did Lyons for silk goods. Strasbourg and other eastern frontier cities prospered as entrepôts, as the Rhine traffic and the trade it provided in both legitimate and contraband goods more than doubled in the years 1806–10.

One serious and adverse effect of the Blockade on France arose from Napoleon's attempts to enforce it throughout Europe. These attempts pushed the country into disastrous new conflicts, most particularly in Spain and in Russia (see pages 25 and 28) and left France weakened militarily, economically and politically and Napoleon's fortunes in decline.

Another serious effect of the Blockade was that it led to the bourgeoisic's withdrawal of their support for Napoleon. This came about as a result of the disastrous economic collapse in France which began in 1810. It was due to numerous causes, including the cost of Napoleon's wars which had become more expensive and less profitable, over-speculation in goods smuggled through the blockade, a public panic to unload old, soon-to-be worthless coins and the hoarding of new-minted francs, and the collapse of several banking houses outside France in which Parisian bankers had invested heavily. While wages had remained steady the cost of raw materials had risen in the years leading up to 1810 and many small firms had borrowed large sums from the banks to survive. When their loans were called in they could not repay their debts and widespread bankruptcies followed. Unemployment rose steeply throughout France.

The crisis was made worse by a very poor harvest in 1811, and a sharp rise in food prices, over 50 per cent in most areas. The government introduced controls on grain and on the sale of bread, and distributed millions of bowls of free vegetable soup and bread substitutes in an attempt to alleviate the hardship, but not until the harvest of 1812 did the situation begin to improve for the majority of people.

Most of the bourgeoisie ignored the original causes of the economic crisis as well as the effect of natural disasters in prolonging it – apart from the bad harvest, there had been a cyclone which devastated the silk producing areas. Instead they put all blame and responsibility for the depression of 1810–11 directly on the workings of the Continental Blockade, and therefore on Napoleon who had introduced it. They had begun by approving his protectionist policy as being to their advantage, but when it no longer proved profitable to them, they abandoned him. He had lost his chief supporters. Even when he more or less abandoned the Blockade in a welter of special export licences, they did not return to his side, but remained markedly indifferent to his subsequent fate and to that of his régime in 1814.

## c)  On Culture

Culturally Napoleon's legacy to France is not inspiring. Even allowing for the stifling effect of his policies of propaganda and indoctrination, he was not much concerned with the arts, literature, sculpture, painting or drama, except in so far as they glorified himself (see page 88). He closed down most of the theatres in Paris, but rather strangely, took the company of the *Théâtre Francaise* with him to Moscow in 1812. Paris itself changed little under Napoleon. Apart from the addition of a number of triumphal monuments in classical style – the Arc de Triomphe itself, and the column in the Place Vendôme surmounted by a statue of Napoleon in a toga, for instance – it remained in appearance the city of Louis XVI.

The style of the years 1800–15, never called 'Napoleonic' but always 'Empire' (perhaps to emphasise the importance of official art), is seen at its most distinctive in the context of interior decoration where it directly reflects Napoleon's own interests. Its inspiration was from the classical world of Greece and Rome (shades of Alexander and Caesar) or from Egypt, where Napoleon in 1798–9 had uncharacteristically concerned himself as much with deciphering the country's ancient heritage as with the process of conquering it. Inlaid furniture, decorated with mythological figures of all kinds and military emblems, was very much the rage, as were the new, tall looking-glasses seen everywhere. Antiquity, with a touch of the east, dominated not only furnishings but the Empire style of dress favoured by everyone in society except Napoleon. Without regard to fashion he continued to wear, except on state occasions, a battered hat, a long grey overcoat and the green jacket of the Imperial Guard.

### d) On the Geography of France

By the time of Brumaire 'old' France had grown considerably in the ten years since 1789 (see page 57) and with each successive year Napoleon pushed the sphere of French influence further beyond the 'natural frontiers' of the Alps, Pyrenees and Rhine, annexing some states, and turning others into French satellites until in 1811 the Empire reached its greatest extent (see the map on page 26).

Was this expansion in the interests of France or not? The Revolutionary governments had fought since 1792 for foreign recognition of France's 'natural frontiers', which would provide clearly defined and easily defensible borders. Until Napoleon's first Italian campaign, the Republic had not envisaged permanent involvement beyond them.

One of the main features of eighteenth-century diplomacy had been to maintain the balance of power, allowing no one country to dominate all others. Conquests had been returned or divided up between interested parties at the end of a war in order to keep a balance among the major powers. By retaining control over his Italian conquests in 1797 at the peace of Campo Formio instead of arranging an exchange of territory, Napoleon set a pattern of expansion for the future, by which, as far as he was concerned, a French conquest remained a conquest. He never willingly parted with any conquered territory – there could be no negotiated peace settlement to restore a pre-war balance of power. That was never his understanding of the purpose of war. As a result, he committed France to further war in defence of each new conquered territory, in the course of which war more lands would be conquered and the pattern begun again – at least while Napoleon continued winning. When in 1812–13 he stopped doing so, the whole house of cards fell apart.

Continuous war necessarily imposed a strain on French resources, both as regards men and materials. In the days of the Consulate and the early Empire the burdens of conscription and taxation, though heavy, were not excessive. Only about half the men conscripted were actually enrolled in the army – the remainder were exempted because they were married, were only sons, were physically unfit or for other reasons – and the shortfall was made up with auxiliary troops supplied by the satellite countries. In the same way the level of taxation could be kept down, for much of the cost of the war was met by tribute payments from the same source. After 1812 the situation changed. With the loss of the Empire the whole burden of raising and maintaining army after army fell on France. Taxation rose sharply – by between 50 and 100 per cent – at a time when many incomes had fallen as a result of the 1810–11 depression. Conscription of yet another army at the end of 1813 to replace that lost at the battle of Leipzig ran into such difficulties that married men were no longer allowed to claim exemption. It was little comfort to peasant families that the Council of State described this development as 'the hard law of necessity', and there are well-substantiated and horrific accounts of the self-mutilation practiced by many young men in order to escape the army at this time.

* Could the Empire be said to have been of any practical benefit to France itself? It is difficult to find much economic benefit, apart from the acquisition of the Rhinelands. This area where there was compara-tively rapid industrial development soon became the most economically advanced part of France, and its loss in 1815 was a serious blow. For a while from 1806 the protectionist policies of the Continental Blockade brought some commercial advantages to France, but it did not last (see above, page 115) and any other profit from the annexed and satellite states was swallowed up, and more, by the cost of continued war. Napoleon had envisaged an Empire which would be a self-supporting entity, providing for France as well as itself. Events proved him to have been over-optimistic (see chapter 5). The prestige of having the largest European Empire since that of Rome was no compensation to most French subjects for the problems of maintaining it. The glory was bought at too high a price.

Napoleonic France came to an end in 1815. The first Treaty of Paris (1814) pushed the frontiers of France back to those of 1792, the second Treaty of Paris pushed them back to 1790. There was nothing left of the imperial possessions. Even the 'natural frontiers' were lost. No trace of the Empire survived, territorially speaking, but some of the political and social gains of the Revolution and of the Napoleonic era *were* salvaged in the Bourbon restoration settlement.

## 5) What Survived after 1815?

Some of Napoleon's innovations disappeared because they were in-appropriate to the suceeding régime – Louis XVIII, given a free hand, would also probably have preferred to rule as an absolute monarch, but pressure from the allies forced him to give France a limited constitu-tion. Napoleon's centralised and autocratic government structure there-fore disappeared, along with the imperial title, in favour of a (nominal-ly) representative government. However, other institutions remained, including much of his bureaucratic organisation which, like a typical bureaucracy, had increased rapidly in size by 1815. The Ministry of the Interior, for instance, which enjoyed very wide-ranging powers, over-seeing provincial administration, trade, arts and crafts, prisons, public works, education, science, welfare and a host of other topics, had proliferated into a number of departments and bureaux with an ever increasing staff to match. The other civil ministries, a dozen or more of them, had expanded equally rapidly to meet the needs of a government perpetually at war, doubling their staff to a total of around 4000 by the late Empire. This well-organised civil service, headed by specially selected and trained auditors (see page 106), has led one present-day historian to describe Napoleon as 'the orginator of modern centralised bureaucracy in France'.

Members of the imperial nobility kept their titles at the Restoration, the Legion of Honour continued to be awarded, Frenchmen remained equal before the law, and the land settlement was left untouched. The legal codes and much of their judicial organisation remained in being. Today, judges are still appointed for life and the *Code Napoléon* is still the foundation of modern French law, although it was recodified in 1958. The provincial administrative system of prefects, sub-prefects and mayors is still the basis of local government. Most of Napoleon's financial reforms survived, including the Bank of France. So too did the *lycées*, in a demilitarised form; and the Baccalaureate examination introduced in 1809 is still faced by French children at the end of their school life. Although the University itself expired with the Empire, its purpose of supervising and standardising education throughout the country lives on, as does its structure of advanced academies, seen in the modern centralisation of French higher education. In religious life, the Concordat, minus the Imperial Catechism, remained the basis of relations between the French government and the Roman Catholic Church until 1904 when it came to an end with an agreement which totally separated Church and State. In the same year government financial support for Protestant ministers was finally abandoned, as was the government oversight of Jewish synagogues. One or two other innovations, smaller and less important, also survived from the Napoleonic régime. These include the local workers' arbitration board (*conseil de prud'hommes*) which still plays a significant part in industrial relations.

It is worth noting that Napoleon's legacy to France was a civil one. From more than a decade of war he left his country no permanent reminder – except a few triumphal arches and the Legion of Honour.

Whether the overall effect of Napoleon's rule on France was for good or ill is debatable – the strong government, the good order, the glory and prestige which he gave the country must be balanced against the restriction of freedom, and the cost of war, in terms of human suffering and economic hardship, which his régime imposed on the French people. Any judgement on this topic must, of course, reflect the values of the individual making it.

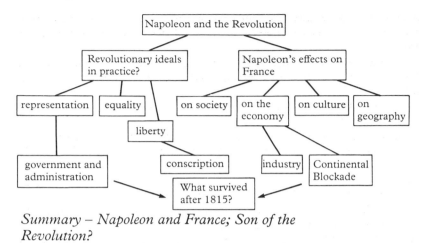

*Summary – Napoleon and France; Son of the Revolution?*

---

***Making notes on '***Napoleon and France: "Son of the Revolution"?*'*

The first half of this chapter covers another popular examination topic – Napoleon's relationship with the Revolution: Did he continue the ideals of the French Revolution? or revert to the policies of the Ancien Régime? Use the following headings to make lists of how Napoleon maintained the principles of the Revolution or departed from them: Representative Government; Administration – staff and organisation; Equality – opportunities and obligations; Liberty – thought, word and deed.

What conclusions about his relationship with the Revolution do you draw from your lists? Was he the 'Son of the Revolution'?

The second half of the chapter deals with the effects of Napoleon's rule on France. Use the headings – society, the economy (including industry and the workings of the Continental Blockade), culture, and geography and make brief notes of his effect in each of these areas of French life. What survived after 1815? What is your evaluation of his overall effect on France? Good or bad; lasting or temporary?

---

***Answering essay questions on '***Napoleon and France: "Son of the Revolution"?*'*

Questions set on this topic are most often based on the proposition that Napoleon was – or was not – heir to the Revolution. To answer the examples given below you will find that you need to use information and ideas from one or more of the preceding chapters as well as from this one.

Unlike those in the previous chapter the following questions are all 'open-ended', calling for discussion and analysis supported by factual information.

1  Do you agree that in 1799 Napoleon brought the French Revolution to an end?
2  Can Napoleon be described as 'son of the French Revolution'?
3  'As heir to the Revolution, he safeguarded its gains for France'. Is this view of Napoleon justified?
4  Did Napoleon's domestic policies succeed because they were largely a return to those of the Ancien Régime?
5  To what extent do the domestic reforms of Napoleon complete the work of the French Revolution?
6  Consider Napoleon's claim to be 'son of the French Revolution' in the light of his statement that 'society is impossible without inequality'.
7  Discuss the view that Napoleon ended the Revolution by destroying its ideals.
8  In terms of liberty and equality did France pay too high a price for stable government under Napoleon?
9  In 1814 Napoleon said 'I have destroyed the Revolution'. Had he?

By its wording each of these questions includes an assumption about Napoleon's relationship with the Revolution, but makes no judgement. It simply asks you to discuss the proposition and by implication to arrive at a reasoned conclusion. (What is the assumption contained in each of the questions?) You should by now be clear in your own mind what *you* consider that relationship to have been. But 'value judgements' of this kind need to be supported, and you will have to explain the reasons for your verdict in the course of your essay.

If, as sometimes happens, questions containing assumptions, instead of being 'open-ended', are written in the 'why', 'how' and 'what' format (see pages 55 and 97) the result is very different. So too must be the approach to answering them. For example:

10  Why did Napoleon abandon the ideals of the Revolution in his domestic policies?
11  How did Napoleon complete the work of the Revolution?

Questions like this can be very dangerous to the unwary. Why is this? What is the best way to deal with them? Examiners are likely to be impressed by an answer which effectively and justifiably queries the assumption and backs up the argument with evidence, *but* this is not a policy to follow unless you are very sure that the assumption is ill-founded!

*Source-based questions on 'Napoleon and France: "Son of the Revolution"?'*

## 1 Napoleon and the Revolution

Re-read carefully pages 100 and 101 and answer the following questions:

a) The second paragraph on page 100 contains a number of statements made by Napoleon about his relationship with the French Revolution. Summarise his views in not more than three sentences. *(6 marks)*

b) In the extract from his speech to the Council in 1812 (page 100), explain what is meant by popular sovereignty and why Napoleon is opposed to it. On what grounds does he attack the idea of parliamentary government on this occasion? What reason did he give on other occasions for disliking it? In the last sentence (lines 8–9) what assumptions does he make about himself and his régime? Are they correct? *(8 marks)*

c) Explain what is meant in the first extract on page 101 by (i) the Revolution being 'accomplished' and (ii) 'the arch of the alliance'. Comment on the last two sentences (lines 8–12). *(8 marks)*

d) Is Napoleon justified in making the statements contained in the second extract on page 101? Explain your answer. *(8 marks)*

e) What light do the extracts (pages 100–101) throw on the character of Napoleon? *(10 marks)*

# CHAPTER 8

# The Napoleonic Legend

When Napoleon died on St Helena in May 1821 he lay in state for two days and was then buried on the island, carried to his anonymous grave on the shoulders of the British soldiers who had been his guards. At the time his death caused little stir in London. 'Nobody talks of it; the only feeling is pleasure that we are saved the expense of keeping him', it was reported. But this dismissal of Napoleon was premature. He was to live on in the 'Napoleonic legend' of which he himself had been the chief architect, and on which others were to build after his death.

## 1 The Legend Begins

The beginnings of the Legend can be traced back, before the successful *coup* of Brumaire, to the string of dazzling victories won by the young Napoleon in Italy in 1796-7 – at Castiglioni, Arcola, Lodi, Rivoli and Mantua – and to the use which he made of them and of the Peace of Campo Formio (see page 21). Sensational as his part in these events was, it was exaggerated and dramatised further, then and later by writers, including Napoleon himself, who described it, and by artists who depicted it.

During this first Italian campaign, Napoleon began a lifelong use of propaganda. As well as making proclamations and issuing orders of the day, he published newsheets, full of disinformation, intended to boost army morale, and to dishearten the enemy. These newsheets were widely circulated, and their contents included suitably embellished reports or bulletins on the progress of the war, written by Napoleon himself. He also sent senior officers to Paris in relays to report personally to the Directory on his victories, making sure that their tales lost nothing in the telling, and that the news was passed on to the Paris press. When he returned to France in 1797 he was greeted as a hero. The *Institut de France*, the leading scientific association in Europe, honoured Napoleon by admitting him to their mathematics division, and everywhere he went he was fêted. At a splendid ceremony in the Luxembourg Palace he personally handed over the Treaty of Campo Formio to the Directors. One eyewitness wrote that 'However great Napoleon's vanity, it must have been well satisfied; all classes united to welcome him home . . . [for] he was seen as a pure and mighty colossus of glory'. The Napoleonic legend had begun.

* Official painters were recruited later to portray Napoleon and his régime in the most flattering light. In the dynamic, romanticised portrait of Napoleon on the bridge at Arcola by Gros, he is the dashing young hero and leader of men, physically quite unlike his real appearance. In the same way he was idealised in the popular painting of

the signing of the treaty of Campo Formio, where a slim and elegant young man stands centre stage, forcefully dictating terms to a number of elderly and subservient-looking negotiators seated around him.

*Napoleon on St Helena*

Compliant painters who were willing to allow themselves a large amount of artistic licence proved extremely useful to Napoleon, tailoring official portraits and recording state events in the way best suited for use as propaganda. Jacques-Louis David, the chief court painter, when called upon to portray Napoleon's crossing of the Alps in the second Italian campaign of 1800, was ordered to show the heroic First Consul 'calm, on a fiery horse' at the head of his men. This he accomplished with great aplomb, although it was common knowledge that Napoleon had travelled on a mule, plodding along some way to the rear of the main army. Napoleon had refused even to sit for David on this occasion, telling him that it was more important to immortalise his spirit of genius than to capture his exact likeness. It was not until long after Napoleon's death that a more realistic version of the scene was painted by a later artist (see pages 125 and 126).

Large-scale paintings, like the four great representations of the Imperial Coronation in 1804 by David, provided not only a record of

*Napoleon Crossing the Alps by Jacques-Louis David*

*Napoleon Crossing the Alps by Paul Delacroche*

the event, but were a propaganda exercise to impress on those not present in Notre Dame the solemnity and splendour of the occasion and the reality of the reconciliation between Church and State. The Romantic painting by Gros of the indecisive battle of Eylau, fought in a snowstorm in February 1807, was, in its way, also a propaganda piece. Its version of the battlefield in no way evokes the horrific reality of the 40,000 French and Russian dead, 'the snow, stained everywhere with blood . . . mounds of a hundred bloody corpses on the side of a hill . . . horses wounded and crippled but still alive, waiting until hunger caused them to fall on to the piles of dead'.

\* Misrepresentation was not the sole prerogative of the artist; it had its literary forms. Throughout his career Napoleon continued the practice of disseminating false reports which he had begun during his first Italian campaign. The battle of Eylau is a good example. It was the first battle in which some of his troops had run away, and his losses among the remainder of the army had been high, yet he managed by skilful manipulation of the facts to make it appear not a drawn encounter but a French victory. He denied Russian accounts of the engagement, dictating 'an eye-witness account, translated from the German' as the version he wished to go down into history, sending home specially commissioned pictures of the action, and writing the inevitable bulletins in which he initially falsified the number of French dead, substituting 2,000 for the real figure of 20,000. He finished by publishing the almost certainly apochryphal 'last words of a French officer killed in the battle'. (They bear a close resemblance to other 'last words' used in earlier bulletins.) 'I die content, since victory is ours . . . Tell the Emperor I have only one regret – that in a few moments I shall be beyond doing anything more in his service or for the glory of France'. There could be no place in the legend for a drawn battle, any more than for a defeat.

In the wake of other battles, bulletins often fulfilled for Napoleon the twin purposes of arousing national enthusiasm and encouraging hatred of the enemy. In any event they paid little heed to the truth. Writing after Austerlitz, for instance, Napoleon described the 'horrible spectacle' of the retreat under artillery fire of 20,000 Russians, who, driven back, were drowned in an 'immense lake' amidst heartrending screams 'which still ring in our ears'. The whole event has to be pure invention, for the lake (which far from immense, was quite small) was drained soon after the battle and only a few cannon, 150 dead horses and three bodies were found. The whole account was intended to throw disgrace on the British, 'those perfidious islanders who are responsible' and ended with the malediction, 'May the cowardly oligarchs in London be visited with punishment for so much suffering!' After the retreat from Moscow it was of course the Russian winter which, unjustly, (see page 30) was apportioned the entire blame for the destruction of the *Grande Armée*. There always had to be a scapegoat to hand. In his very last bulletin, issued after Waterloo, Napoleon complained that Wellington, 'who ought not to have won', owed his victory only to 'a sudden and unexplained panic terror which swept the entire field, so that in a moment the [French] army had become nothing but a confused mass'.

However, the most blatant example in any bulletin of tampering with the truth must be that written by Napoleon after the battle of Marengo in June 1800. This 'official' account is full of inconsistencies which turn a near run defeat into an easy victory. Much worse, though, it quite cynically took away from the two army commanders, who broke the enemy line and won the battle, the credit due to them for the victory, and appropriated it to Napoleon himself. A charitable explanation put forward by one historian is that, as he was still uncertain of his position as First Consul, he felt he should, for the good of France, take every opportunity to maintain public belief in his invincibility and so maintain faith in the government, but it seems most probable that his motives were more concerned with his own advancement. He certainly reaped the rewards of his duplicity: 'The victory anthems and the mood of triumphant joy spread throughout France. The First Consul . . . returned to Paris, able to say with justice like Caesar *veni, vidi, vici*. A campaign so short and so decisive, so brilliant, had never previously been witnessed'.

As well as by the positive manipulation of public opinion in his favour, he sought to control men's minds in other ways: through education, 'above all we must secure unity – we must be able to cast a whole generation in the same mould'; through the Imperial catechism with its cult of the Emperor, 'he defends the state by the strength of his arm; he has become the Lord's Annointed', and through propaganda of all kinds. He also exercised a negative influence by the use of censorship and the suppression of freedom of expression. The bulletins and articles published in the government newspaper, *Le Moniteur*, not only propounded the official and accepted view of events, but by 1806 had become the only news source on political or military matters available to the French people. No discussion of perceptions other than Napoleon's was possible when there were no other views available to discuss.

## 2 The Legend Develops

In exile on St Helena Napoleon spent a large part of his time perfecting his life story in order, as one historian puts it, 'to provide a portrait in which there was nought but unblemished beauty, endearing humanity, greatness and virtue'. From the moment of his arrival on St Helena he seems to have been determined to make the best of his opportunities for self-advertisement. As he pointed out to his companions, 'Our situation here may even have its attractions; the whole world is looking at us; we are martyrs in an immortal cause'. He began by dictating his own *Memoirs*, but these, concerned largely with details of his early campaigns and that of Waterloo, are conspicuously dull. Much more interesting are the reminiscences, diaries and journals written by his companions on St Helena, which record in considerable detail Napoleon's conversations and discourses set against the background of everyday life at Longwood, the house where he lived on the island.

The first and most influential of these documentary sources, published only a year after Napoleon's death, was the *Mémoriale de Ste. Helénè*, the best seller of the nineteenth century. Written by the Comte de Las Cases as a record of conversations with Napoleon between 1815 and 1818, when Las Cases returned to France, it is probably the most important single element in the later development of the Legend. Despite being described as 'an effusion of sentimental old French twaddle' by one reader soon after publication, it has been extensively, and sometimes uncritically, used ever since as the chief guide in evaluating Napoleon's historical importance.

The *Mémoriale* and to some extent the journals by O'Meara and others need to be used with caution. They all suffer from the same defects – that they were intended from the first for publication and were written by men devoted to Napoleon. (Three private journals, never meant for other eyes, present a much more unvarnished picture of Napoleon, but have only become available for study comparatively recently and have not so far been greatly used by historians and biographers.) Napoleon encouraged his companions to write down verbatim everything he said, or more often dictated to them, by promising quite correctly that the records they were compiling would make their fortunes when published after his death.

Las Cases, whose *Mémoriale* runs to around 500,000 words, based his work on notes made at the time, but seems to have edited them extensively before publication, smoothing Napoleon's usual abrupt phrases and fiery rhetoric into a well-rounded literary style much more like that of Las Cases' own. Opinions vary about how accurately Napoleon's actual words were recorded by any of the diarists; but even if every word *were* reproduced exactly as spoken, 'whether it is all true is quite another thing!' as an early critic said after reading the journal kept by O'Meara, Napoleon's doctor on the island.

Did Napoleon convince himself that his version of events was correct – a case of self-deception – or did he knowingly twist the truth for political reasons – a case of intentional duplicity? No doubt, like all great men fallen from power he needed to bolster up his self-esteem and justify himself to the world, to gloss over his failures, to excuse his mistakes and to explain his motives. But most historians now believe that, in the light of the political climate of the post-Waterloo years – the years of the Bourbon restoration, the Holy Alliance, and the triumph of reaction – he set out to change the public perception of his role, from that of a dictator to that of the longtime, albeit unrecognised, champion of liberalism and nationalism. As in effect a prisoner of the Holy Alliance, how could he be otherwise than a liberal?

This transformation of his public image required a careful refashioning of his career; but, once achieved and the finished result brought before an admiring world, his historical reputation would, he expected, be assured and the eventual succession of his son made a real possibility. In the course of his reported conversations with Las Cases and the others he pointed to the liberal constitution of the Hundred Days, and declared that his previous autocratic rule had been forced upon him by circumstances, and was in any case no more than a temporary measure needed to enable him as a true patriot to defend France against her enemies. 'If I had won in 1812, my constitutional reign would have begun then. Had I reigned 20 years longer I would have shown the difference between a constitutional emperor and a king of France'. As 'the natural mediator in the struggle of the past [i.e. the old ruling families of Europe] against the Revolution' he had brought together monarchy and liberalism. He was not warlike; he had always wanted peace. It was only the old dynasties who had imposed war upon him. He had been forced to stop them destroying the Revolutionary gains in France, and to liberate and unify the peoples of Europe who were still being oppressed by feudal governments. 'Each of my victories was a diplomatic step on my road towards restoring peace to Europe . . . after every victory I always offered a general peace.' If he had been given time, the 'people's Emperor' would have 'divided Europe into national states, freely formed and free internally . . . a United States of Europe would have become a possibility' in a new era of peaceful economic co-operation.

## 3 The Legend Gains Momentum

After Napoleon's death in 1821 the legend did not end, but gained momentum (despite an official ban until 1830 on the publication in France of any material favourable to him). Indeed, it can be argued that one of the major factors in the rapid growth of the legend in the 1820s and 1830s was Napoleon's own downfall and lonely death in exile. His carefully staged and emotional farewell to the Imperial Guard at Fontainbleau in April 1814 appealed to the poets and artists of the Romantic Age, who produced some appallingly sentimental versions of the event. Chateaubriand, one of the outstanding French literary figures of the early nineteenth century, who had always been extremely hostile to Napoleon, pointed out how easy it was to glorify Napoleon once he was dead and his ill-doings a thing of the past:

1 It is the fashion of the day to magnify Napoleon's victories. Gone are the sufferers, and the victims' curses, their cries of pain, their howls of anguish are heard no more . . . no longer are parents

imprisoned for their sons, nor a whole village punished for the
5 desertion of a conscript . . . no longer are the conscription lists
stuck up at street corners . . . It is forgotten that the people, the
court, the generals, the friends of Napoleon had all become weary
of his oppression and his conquests.

And people *were* forgetting that Napoleon had been a dictator, now
that they were faced with the dull Bourbon court, the *emigrés* and the
priests and the end of any further glory for France. In the seeming
dreariness of everyday life, the remembrance of his final defeat was
forgotten and only the brilliance of his victories remained, a brilliance
which seemed in retrospect to have exalted all France. The soldier,
staunch Republican and author Stendhal, who had muttered about
'trampled liberty' and complained about imperial trappings during
Napoleon's lifetime, afterwards attempted to explain why he and his
contemporaries had not actively opposed Napoleon's dictatorship:

1 In 1794 we had no form of religion – our spirit expressed itself in
  the idea of *serving our country* . . . This idea *was* our religion.
  When Napoleon appeared [1796–7] and put an end to the series of
  defeats to which we were exposed by the feeble government of the
5 Directory we considered his dictatorship solely in terms of its
  *military value* to France; he won victories for us and we judged all
  his actions by the standards of the religion which we felt in our
  hearts: what we valued in his dictatorship was *service being done to
  our country* . . . Thus it was that there were men who genuinely
10 loved Napoleon and who would admit no other criterion than that
  of 'serving the country' for judging the Emperor's actions.

By the 1830s the Romantics were looking back to a 'Golden Age' that
never was, and mourning the so-called 'martyrdom' of the last days on
St Helena. The doctor, O'Meara, was responsible through his journal
'*Voice from St Helena*' for adding to the Legend this element of the
martyr 'chained like Prometheus to a rock' or, 'Christ-like, crucified by
the allies', and left there to suffer a lonely death. It is an interesting
question whether, if Napoleon had been allowed to retire after Waterloo into private life in England or in the United States, as he asked
permission to do, the Legend would have developed and survived as it
did.
A 'bored generation', born too late to have fought in his wars, found
a hero in Napoleon, emphasising his conquests and the glory which he
brought to France, while ignoring the deaths and the loss of political
liberty which were their accompaniment. Nostalgia knew no bounds as
writers began to vie with one another in fulsome adulation. 'The
blessed poets shall kneel before you', wrote Victor Hugo, 'the clouds
which have obscured your glory have passed, and nothing will ever dim

its true lustre again'. Novelists filled their books with idealistic young heroes whose Bible was the *'Mémoriale'*; cheap copies of popular and sentimental Napoleonic songs sold in their hundreds of thousands, and disaffected young men, sporting shaggy moustaches in imitation of those worn by the Imperial Guard, listened with envy to the campaign tales told by Napoleon's old soldiers. It was all very Romantic and unreal, but the high spot was still to come.

## 4 The Accolade

In his will Napoleon had asked that 'my remains rest on the banks of the Seine, among the French people that I loved so well'. In a bid to court popularity, Louis-Philippe, the last king of France, decided to fulfil Napoleon's wishes and restore him to Paris. In October 1840, almost 25 years to the day since Napoleon had landed on St Helena, a French ship arrived there, with British permission, to take him home. The body, apparently untouched by time, was prepared for the long sea voyage back to France by being placed in a new coffin covered with a pall embroidered with the initial 'N' and a crown. In December the cortege arrived in Paris and with great ceremony was escorted in procession to the Invalides, where the bier, surrounded by Napoleonic relics (his hat, his sword worn at Austerlitz, his insignia of the Legion of Honour), was put under the initial guardianship of a man who had enlisted as a drummer-boy in the *Grande Armée* of 1805 and had followed the Emperor ever after. With the final re-interment of the body in a magnificent sarcophagus below the dome of the Invalides, the Napoleonic legend reached its high point. Hero-worship merged imperceptibly into quasi-religious veneration, reaching perhaps its most extreme manifestation in the late 1890s. Then, on the basis of a casual remark by Napoleon that he had the 'gift of electrifying men', he was credited by some with supernatural powers and hailed as a 'Teacher of Energy' (*Professeur d'Energie*), able 'to enlarge the souls' of those who visted his tomb.

More prosaically, one evening in 1855 Queen Victoria and the Emperor Napoleon III stood together in the Invalides. The Queen put her hand on the shoulder of the small boy beside her. 'Kneel down', she said, 'before the tomb of the great Napoleon'. How Napoleon would have relished the sight of the future Edward VII kneeling before him – 'Perfidious Albion' humbled, if only symbolically, and Waterloo in some degree avenged.

After the death of his son, the King of Rome, in 1832 the 'friendly' version of Napoleon's career was taken up and publicised by two of his nephews. The first of these was the politically ambitious Louis-Napoleon, now head of the family (see the family tree on page 140). He staged unsuccessful *coups* in 1836 and 1840, in the course of which he proclaimed that he 'represented . . . a principle, a cause and a defeat:

the principle is the sovereignty of the people, the cause is the cause of
the Empire, and the defeat is Waterloo'. In his *Napoleonic Ideas* he set
out in detail the Legend view of the First Empire, describing it as an
example to be followed. When as Napoleon III he became Emperor in
his turn, standing for 'order and authority, religion, the welfare of the
people and . . . for national dignity' many, therefore, expected that he
would prove a reincarnation of the Napoleon of the Legend. This did
not happen, and with the collapse of his régime in 1870 the Legend
suffered an eclipse; but only temporarily. The dullness of the succeed-
ing Third Republic soon led to a revival of interest in past glories and
brought the Legend back into favour, not least because of the
enthusiastic and unquestioning support which it received from the
second Bonaparte nephew, Prince Napoléon. He represents the Legend
in its most extreme form in which the Hero can do no wrong – 'to
defend Napoleon's memory is to serve France. The glory of Napoleon
is a national possession: whoever touches it defaces the nation itself'.

## 5 Napoleon's View of History

Napoleon never seems to have had any serious doubts about the verdict
of history on his career. This was not surprising as he took great pains
to provide historians with records favourable to it, both before and after
1815. It was typical of him that, glancing through old copies of the
official, government sponsored newspaper, *Le Moniteur*, he expressed
his approval: 'These are invariably favourable to me alone. Really
talented and careful historians will write history with official documents. Now these documents are full of me; it is their testimony I
solicit and invoke'.

A year or two later on St Helena he called on historians as witnesses
for the defence:

1   I have no fear whatever about my fame. Posterity will do me
    justice. The truth will be known . . . I am not uneasy about the
    result. Had I succeeded I should have died with the reputation of
    the greatest man who ever existed. As it is, though I have failed, I
5   shall be considered as an extraordinary man . . . From nothing I
    raised myself to be the most powerful monarch in the world . . .
    The historian of the Empire . . . will have an easy task, for the
    facts speak for themselves, they shine like the sun . . . On what
    point could I be assailed on which a historian could not defend
10  me? For my intentions? As to these I can be absolved. For my
    despotism? But it can be demonstrated that dictatorship was
    absolutely necessary. Will it be said that I restricted liberty? It
    can be proved that licentiousness and anarchy still threatened
    liberty. Shall I be accused of being too fond of war? It can be
15  shown I was always attacked first . . . Shall I be blamed for my

ambition? . . . my ambition was of the highest and noblest kind
that ever perhaps existed! that of establishing and consecrating
the rule of reason and the exercise and enjoyment of all the human
faculties! Here the historian will probably feel compelled to regret
20 that such an ambition was not fulfilled.

## 6  Historians' Views of Napoleon

One of the very few intellectuals to stand up to Napoleon during his
time in power was the Catholic nobleman Chateaubriand. By publishing an article in 1807 attacking the Emperor as a tyrant who would
have to appear before the judgement seat of history, and following it up
in 1814 with a pamphlet denouncing him as a destroyer of men and a
suppressor of freedom, Chateaubriand may be said to be the first of the
thousands of historians who have given their verdict 'for or against'
Napoleon. It is fitting therefore that he should occupy the first pages of
the Dutch historian Geyl's major survey of the differing views of
French historians, and be closely followed by a fellow intellectual,
Madame de Staël, whose account of Napoleon was published soon after
her death in 1818. It was just as critical, just as damning as Chateaubriand's, but had that extra dimension of a historical perspective, setting
Napoleon in his time and place, measuring him against events – and
finding him wanting. Geyl even goes so far as to suggest that 'later
writers, though capable of finer shades and possessing a far richer store
of data, can only elaborate her themes'.

Within a few years, French histories of Napoleon were multiplying
rapidly. One of these, commissioned by Napoleon himself in his will,
was a well documented multi-volume work, which the author confide-
ntly stated contained so faithful an account of the real facts that future
historians would have no need to investigate further. Others might
write with better grace, but would find nothing significant to add. He
would have been very affronted to have known that he was merely one
of the early participants in a continuing historical argument which two
centuries later shows no signs of abating.

What makes Napoleon and his times so inviting to the historian that
more than 200,000 books and articles have been written about him
since his death? Yet from all this mass of paper no standard view of
Napoleon, no definitive life has appeared. Historians are still as
basically divided into 'admirers' and 'detractors', 'for' or 'against', as
they were in the early nineteenth century; but within that broad
division their views of Napoleon are legion. Was he 'the heir of the
Revolution', or an unprincipled adventurer; a reformer, or a dictator; a
liberal, a nationalist, a tool of the bourgeoisie, a military genius, an
ogre; was he the patriot who said 'always France first'? or the ambitious
egoist who said 'France needs me more than I need her'? Or was he
something of them all? From the mass of evidence available, as one

modern British historian has perceptively written, 'each writer, and indeed each reader constructs his own Napoleon'. To quote Geyl again,

1 We cannot see the past in a single communicable picture, except from a point of view, which implies a choice, a personal perspective. It is impossible that two historians, especially two living in different periods should see any historical personality in the same
5 light. The greater the political importance of an historical character, the more impossible this is.

With as many-sided a personality as Napoleon – so given to making entirely contradictory statements about himself, his actions and his beliefs, so differently perceived by friends and enemies – the business of the historian to explain, interpret, and assess his motives and intentions is extremely difficult.

## 7 Conclusion

It is no longer fashionable, historically speaking, to place a single individual centre stage, dominating events; modern historians generally adopt a broader, less personality-based view of their subject. The 'great men' school of historical writing pioneered by the nineteenth-century historian, Carlyle, is out of date; the title 'Napoleon the Great' no longer current.

1 A man is only a man; his power is nothing if circumstances are not favourable. If I had not appeared someone else would have done the same thing. I consider that I count for no more than half in the battles I have won. The general's name is hardly worth
5 mentioning, for the fact is it is the army which wins the battle.

These remarks by Napoleon may of course have been simply a display of false modesty, but, if not, they were surprising and untypical ones for him to have made. In one sense of course he did only make use of circumstances, which *were* favourable to him; but without his particular personality, the mixture of drive and determination, ambition and ability, added to his powers of leadership, the course of events must certainly have been different. It is difficult to imagine otherwise.

Was he a 'great' man, a 'great' ruler? Believing that greatness in a ruler inevitably implied successful military offensives, Napoleon modelled himself on three great conquerors of the past each of whom had in turn carved out an empire: Alexander, Caesar and above all Charlemagne, whose successor he liked to believe himself to be and whose relics he collected. At the time of the coronation he tried hard to borrow the antique regalia believed to have been used by Charlemagne, but the Habsburg Emperor would not lend them to a rival. As well as in the guise of victorious leader, Napoleon saw himself following in the footsteps of Charlemagne in another way – as a great lawmaker. Napoleon had codified the customary and other laws of France as Charlemagne had codified the tribal laws of Germany. The proudest achievement of his career was, he declared, the Civil Code, (the *Code Napoléon*), the introduction of which into the conquered territories united in one legal system all the countries of the Empire.

What did his contemporaries think on the question of his greatness? Metternich, the Austrian Foreign Minister and implacable enemy of France, in *A Portrait of Napoleon Bonaparte* published in 1820 set himself to discuss 'Whether Napoleon did in fact deserve to be called a great man?' He decides that 'it would be impossible to dispute his great qualities who rising from obscurity, had become the strongest and most powerful of men', but considers that Napoleon must be seen against the background of the age. If the era of the Revolution was a glorious one, the fact that Napoleon was able to take and keep first place in it for 15 years, means that he was 'certainly one of the greatest men who have ever appeared'; but if, as Metternich himself believes, the era was one of general dissolution then 'the splendour of his success diminishes' and 'we are in no danger of exaggerating Napoleon's grandeur, while still acknowledging that there was something extraordinary and imposing in his career'. Other contemporaries, friends and enemies alike, saw a downward trend in his career, running parallel to the deterioration in his character and intellect beginning in 1808 and becoming more marked from 1812 owards. Most thought that Napoleon had started well, 'the beginning of his career stamped with greatness because in his rapid ascent from obscurity to the pinnacle of glory and power, he had recourse only to what was great about him', but that the end of his career was 'miserable because his heart was hard and his spirit petty'. Power had corrupted him and he would 'go down to posterity as a man who, having more good at his disposal than any other potentate of a former age, had actually applied his immense means to the production of a greater share of mischief and misery to his fellow creatures – one who, on the basis of French liberty, might have founded that of every other state in Europe'.

What do present-day historians think on the question of Napoleon's greatness? Every possible shade of opinion can be found in modern histories and biographies (see Further Reading page 144), from the 'great bad man' to the 'great and the good', depending on the criteria used to assess his achievements, and even more on the writer's own point of view. Fascinated or repelled, it is impossible to stand aside, unaffected, by Napoleon. He dominated an age and a continent, out-lived his death, and exercises still the wits of historians to unravel his story.

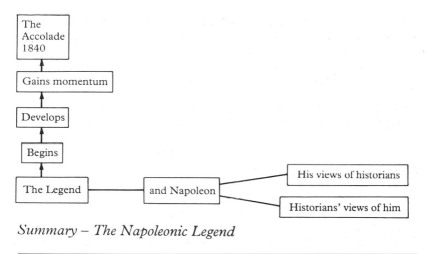

*Summary – The Napoleonic Legend*

---

### Making Notes on 'The Napoleonic Legend'

It is very unlikely that you will be faced with an examination question based directly on the information contained in this chapter, and you will probably decide that there is no need to make detailed notes on it. But the Legend *is* important for the effect it has had on Napoleon's historical reputation and you need to be able to recognise the bias which results when uncritical use is made by historians or biographers of the government propaganda put out by Napoleon himself or of the St Helena writings of Las Cases, O'Meara and others.

In this connection you should be clear in your mind on the following points:

1  What was the purpose of Napoleon's official propaganda prior to 1815? What forms did it take? (A quick look back at chapter 7, pages 87–92, might be helpful here.)

2  Why and in what ways did he try to change his image in his St Helena reminiscences? Was it a convincing performance?

At the end of chapter 1 it was suggested that you should compile your own pen-portrait of Napoleon as you worked through the rest of the book. Now is the time to make your final assessment. Are you 'for' or 'against'? Why?

---

### Answering essay questions on 'Napoleon, France and Europe'

It is not unknown for examiners to set extremely general questions on Napoleon. Typical of these are:

1 Why was Napoleon so successful and for so long?
2 What was the basis of Napoleon's power?
3 When and how did Napoleon's power decline?

All these briefly worded questions appear deceptively simple and superficially attractive. The snag lies in their broad scope for none of them is specific to France or to Europe. To answer them well presupposes not only a sufficient knowledge of both domestic and imperial affairs but the ability to select what is relevant and to present a coherent answer within the limited time and space of an examination essay. Unless you are confident of your ability to do this under pressure, it is better to avoid questions of this kind.

Other, rather more structured general questions are often framed around quotations. For example:

4 'Napoleon's achievements at home are more significant than his conquests abroad'. Is this a balanced judgement?
5 'A liberaliser and moderniser' in France and in Europe. Can this view of Napoleon be justified?
6 'His legal and administrative reforms are his chief claim to fame'. Consider this verdict on Napoleon's career.
7 'A gust of modernisation blew through Europe in the wake of Napoleon'. Discuss this comment on the Grand Empire.
8 'I have governed for the nation and in its interests'. Is Napoleon's view of his régime realistic?

While these questions, too, are wide ranging, the basic pattern of the answer is set out for you. Do not be put off by the quotation. If you are uncertain what the examiner is asking, just turn the quotation into a direct question. For instance question 5 above would then read 'Are his legal and administrative reforms Napoleon's chief claim to fame?' so becoming an 'open-ended' question of the type discussed on page 8.

---

*Source-based questions on 'The Napoleonic Legend'*

### 1 Portraits

Look carefully at the illustrations on the front cover and page 124 and answer the following questions:

a) The cover portrait was painted to order soon after Napoleon came to power. Assuming that it was completed to his satisfaction, what can be deduced from it about how he wished to appear as a public figure? (*4 marks*)
b) The drawing of Napoleon was made on St Helena towards the end of his life. Contrast his appearance with that above. What is the general impression created by the drawing? (*6 marks*)

**2 Fact and Fiction**
Look carefully at the two pictures of Napoleon (pages 125 and 126) and answer the following questions:
a) The picture of Napoleon crossing the Alps in 1800 riding a horse was painted soon after the event, the one of him doing the same riding a mule is from about 1840. Comment on the differences between the two portrayals. (*6 marks*)
b) Which painting would not have been to Napoleon's satisfaction? Why? (*4 marks*)

**3 Napoleon and Historians**
Carefully read the extracts on pages 133 and 134 and answer the following questions:
a) What is Napoleon's view of historians and their work? (*5 marks*)
b) Assess the defence of his actions made by Napoleon in the longer extract. Illustrate your answer with specific examples. (*10 marks*)

Carlo Maria Bonaparte = Marie Letizia (Madame Mère)
died 1785 / died 1836

**JOSEPH**
King of Naples to 1808
King of Spain 1808-13
died 1844

Vicomte de Beauharnais = Josephine Tascher de la Pagerie (1) = **NAPOLEON** (2) = Marie Louise of Austria married 1810
died 1814
First Consul 1799–1804
Emperor of the French 1804-15
died 1821

Eugène de Beauharnais Viceroy of Italy — Hortense*

**Napoleon** King of Rome died 1832

**LUCIEN** Prince of Canino died 1840

Elise Duchess of Lucca died 1820

**LOUIS** King of Holland 1806-10 died 1846 = Hortense*

Charles Louis Napoleon (Napoleon III) died 1873

Pauline died 1825

Caroline died 1839 = Joachim MURAT King of Naples 1808

**JEROME** King of Westphalia 1806-14 died 1860 = ...

Napoleon Joseph Charles (Prince Napoleon) died 1891

*Napoleonic Family Tree*

# Chronological Table

1769   15 August, Napoleon born at Ajaccio, Corsica
1784   Entered *École Militaire* Paris
1785   Commissioned as artillery officer
1793   In command artillery at siege of Toulon
        Became involved in Corsican affairs and enjoyed considerable
        political patronage
1795   Helped put down Royalist rising in Paris
1796   February, appointed commander Army of Italy
        March, married Josephine de Beauharnais
        May, victory at Lodi; entered Milan
        August, victory at Castiglione
        October, victory at Arcola
1797   January, victory at Rivoli
        February, captured Mantua
        April, armistice with Austrians at Leoben
        October, Peace of Campo Formio
1798   Second Coalition (1798–1802)
        May, embarked for Egypt
        July, battle of the Pyramids
        August, French fleet destroyed by Nelson in Aboukir Bay
1799   February, siege of Acre
        July, defeated Ottomans at Aboukir
        August, abandoned army and left Egypt
        October, reached France
        9–10 November, *coup d'état* of 18–19 Brumaire
        December, Constitution of year VIII; Napoleon First Consul
1800   February, Bank of France created
        June, battle of Marengo
        December, battle of Hohenlinden
1801   Peace of Lunéville
        July, Concordat with Pope
1802   Peace of Amiens ended war of Second Coalition
        August, Napoleon appointed First Consul for life
1803   Invasion of England planned and abandoned
1804   *Code Napoléon* introduced
        March, Duc d'Enghien kidnapped and executed
        May, Senate proclaimed Napoleon Emperor of the French
        December, Coronation in Notre Dame in presence of Pope
1805   Third Coalition (1805)
        May, crowned King of Italy in Milan
        August, invaded Germany
        October, victory at Ulm but French fleet defeated at Trafalgar

December, battle of Austerlitz
1806    July, creation of Confederation of the Rhine
October, battle of Jena
November, Continental Blockade introduced
1807    February, indecisive battle of Eylau
June, battle of Friedland
July, Treaty of Tilsit with Tsar Alexander; Grand Duchy of Warsaw established
November, Lisbon occupied
December, Continental Blockade extended
1808    July, Joseph Bonaparte made King of Spain
1809    July, battle of Wagram; Papal States invaded and Pope taken prisoner by Napoleon
October, Peace of Vienna
December, divorce of Josephine
1810    April, marriage to Marie-Louise of Austria
July, Louis Bonaparte dismissed as King of Holland; Holland annexed to France
1811    March, birth of Napoleon's son, the King of Rome
1812    Russian campaign
September, battle of Borodino; entry into Moscow
October–December retreat from Moscow
1813    Fourth Coalition (1813–15)
October, battle of Leipzig; French forced withdraw to the Rhine
December, allied invasion of France
1814    March, fall of Paris
April, abdication by Napoleon
May, exiled to Elba
1815    March, escaped from Elba and landed in France; beginning of the 'Hundred Days'
April, promised new parliamentary régime in *Acte Additionel*
June, battles of Quatre Bras and Waterloo; second abdication
October, exile on St Helena began; Las Cases and others wrote the Legend during next five years
1821    5 May, death of Napoleon; buried on St Helena
1832    Death of the King of Rome
1840    December, Napoleon's remains moved from St Helena to *Les Invalides* in Paris and the Napoleonic Legend came of age.

# Glossary

| | |
|---|---|
| **aides** | duties on food and drink |
| **arrondissement** | see département |
| **biens nationaux** | property of the church and emigrés and seized by the state and sold at auction |
| **bourgeoisie** | wealthy urban middle class – (name also given by some French historians to all eighteenth-century property-owners including landowners) |
| **commune** | see département |
| **département** | largest local government territorial division, made up of a collection (arrondissement) of communes, the smallest territorial division |
| **domaine extraordinaire** | a special fund set up in 1810 to deal with the monies levied in the conquered states |
| **emigré** | royalist who went into exile during the revolution |
| **lettres de cachet** | written orders authorising imprisonment without trial |
| **livret** | work permit needed by employee to obtain job |
| **notables** | wealthy landowners and property owners, noble and non-noble, used by Napoleon as government officials |
| **préfet** | government official – successor to the intendant of the Ancien Régime |
| **senatorerie** | estate and revenues granted to favoured senators |

# Further Reading

There is a great, indeed overwhelming wealth of historical writing on Napoleon and his Empire – an estimated 200,000 books and articles have been published on the subject since his death in 1821. The majority of them are of course in French, but there are a good number in English or available in translation. Only a small selection from this extensive literature can be given here, but among books which can be recommended and which cover a wide range of topics and views are:

**I. Collins**, *Napoleon: First Consul and Emperor of the French* (Historical Association 1986). This is a brief pamphlet of less than 20 pages of text, but is nevertheless a stimulating examination of contrasting modern historical views on some aspects of Napoleon's career.

**D. Chandler**, *Napoleon* (Weidenfeld and Nicholson 1973). A good military history, in which chapter 6 summarises the author's mammoth 1000-page *Napoleon's Campaigns* (1966) for the benefit of all but the most dedicated.

**C. Barnett**, *Napoleon* (Allen and Unwin 1978). This is a very well illustrated volume by a military historian strongly anti-Napoleon in outlook, and refreshing for its stringent criticisms of Napoleon's abilities as a soldier. The section on the Russian campaign is particularly illuminating.

**O. Connelly**, *Blundering to Glory* (1988) A not very flattering reappraisal of Napoleon as military leader.

**V. Cronin**, *Napoleon* (Collins 1971). This, in contrast, is a slightly fictionalised, very pro-Napoleon biography. As long as its limitations are recognised (in addition to its bias, there are substantial omissions) it provides a pleasant 'easy-read' introduction to the subject for both student and general reader.

**J.M. Thompson**, *Napoleon* (Blackwell 1952). This typifies the more academic biographical approach, being firmly based on the evidence of Napoleon's own letters. Sadly lacking in maps, or other visual features to enliven its rather old-fashioned format, it is nevertheless well worth reading, or at least dipping into by use of its detailed contents list, for the wealth of interesting information it contains.

**J. Tulard**, *Napoleon – the Myth of the Saviour*, Paris 1977 (English translation Weidenfeld and Nicolson 1984). Not strictly speaking a biography, this is nevertheless an enjoyable book, full of thought-provoking ideas about the rôle of the saviour figure in French history, and including a summary of the author's own research on Napoleonic society. The translation unfortunately leaves a good deal to be desired.

**F. Markham**, *Napoleon* (Wiedenfeld and Nicolson 1963). This is probably still the best all-round biography in English, combining as it does readability with scholarship. Recommended also, especially for a quick preliminary overview, is the same author's brief volume *Napoleon and the Awakening of Europe* (EUP 1958). Distinctly pro-Napoleon.

**D.G. Wright**, *Napoleon and Europe* (Longman 1984). This volume in the Seminar Studies series provides a somewhat sketchy, generally sympathetic introduction to Napoleon and his European Empire, together with a few selected documents and a good annotated bibliography.

**P. Geyl**, *Napoleon: For and Against* (Cape 1949). This is a detailed comparative study of French historians' views on Napoleon, and was, in its time, a seminal work. It has not unfortunately been extended to cover post-1950 French Napoleonic studies, and is therefore now sadly out of date It is, neverthless, still of great interest to the serious student.

**G. Lefebvre**, *Napoleon*, Paris 1935 (English translation, Routledge and Kegan Paul 1969). An excellent and detailed 'life and times', very fairly presented by an eminent Marxist historian. Despite its age, it remains a basic text.

**D.M.G. Sutherland**, *France 1789–1815 Revolution and Counter Revolution* (Fontana 1985). Although this book is mostly concerned with the French Revolution, chapters 9–12 provide an interestingly written, somewhat unconventional view of the Consulate and Empire.

**P. Fregosi**, *Dreams of Empire* (Cardinal 1991). This is a delightfully unconventional book, giving an entertaining, not to say racy, account of Napoleon's pursuit of a colonial empire. The author makes out a case for the resulting near-global conflict to be considered the first genuine world war.

**G. Ellis**, *Napoleonic Empire* (Macmillan 1991) is interesting for the use it makes of European sources and for its emphasis on the importance of recent research especially on the social and economic aspects of Napoleonic France. It provides an opportunity for students and the general reader to learn what is currently being done in Napoleonic studies by European historians, especially those whose work is not available in translation. Has a good, annotated bibliography.

**L. Bergeron**, *France Under Napoleon* Paris, 1972 (English translation, Princeton 1982). Chiefly concerned with social, cultural and economic affairs, and based on the author's own very substantial research, this is a difficult book, made more so by a translation some parts of which are unintelligible.

## Sources on Napoleon, France and Europe

There are a number of English-language documentary collections available. Among those largely concerned with Napoleon's own words, whether spoken or written, are:

**S. de Chair (ed)**, *Napoleon's Memoirs* (Faber and Faber 1948)

**J.C. Herold**, *The Mind of Napoleon* (Columbia University Press 1948)

**J.M. Thompson (ed)**, *Napoleon's Letters* (Dent 1954)

Other more general collections relating to Napoleon and his times include:

**M. Hutt,** *Napoleon* (Spectrum 1972) and

**D. Dowd,** *Napoleon: Was he the heir of the Revolution?* (Krieger 1982)
  Also of interest are a number of eyewitness accounts, especially:

**C. Hibbert (ed),** *A Soldier of the 71st* (Leo Cooper 1975) – a captivating fair-minded account, both touching and humorous, of the Peninsular War and the Waterloo campaign, and

**A. Brett-James (ed),** *Eyewitness Accounts of Napoleon's Defeat in Russia* (Macmillan 1966) – full of scarifying stories of the campaign and the horrors experienced by civilians and soldiers on both sides.


### Acknowledgements

The publishers would like to thank the following for giving permission to use copyright photographs in this book:

Cover, Musée de Liege/Bridgeman Art Library; p. 12, Louvre/Bridgeman Art Library; p. 14, Trustees of the British Museum; p. 124, Mansell Collection; p. 125, The Board of Trustees of the National Museums & Galleries on Merseyside/Walker Art Gallery; p. 126, Charlottenburg Castle, Berlin/Bridgeman Art Library.

# Index

Readers seeking a specific piece of information might find it helpful to consult the table of *Contents* and the *Chronological Table* as well as this brief *Index*.